Living
with Joy

Books by Sanaya Roman

Living with Joy: Keys to Personal Power and Spiritual Transformation
Book I of the Earth Life Series

Personal Power through Awareness: A Guidebook for Sensitive People
Book II of the Earth Life Series

Spiritual Growth: Being Your Higher Self
Book III of the Earth Life Series

Books by Sanaya Roman and Duane Packer, Ph.D.

Opening to Channel: How to Connect with Your Guide

Creating Money: Keys to Abundance

BOOK I EARTH LIFE SERIES

Living with Joy

KEYS TO PERSONAL POWER & SPIRITUAL TRANSFORMATION

Sanaya Roman
CHANNEL FOR ORIN

H J Kramer Inc
Tiburon, California

To all of you awakening to the light within.

H.J. Kramer, Inc., Publishers
P.O. Box 1082
Tiburon, California 94920

Cover painting "Sacred Flame" © 1985 by Judith Cornell, Ph.D.
Book design by Abigail Johnston

First paperback edition 1986
Manufactured in the United States of America
10 9 8 7

ACKNOWLEDGMENTS

To Duane Packer, PhD, for his healing, empowerment, and love; for encouraging me to be all that I can be and for standing beside me with his wise guidance, and for his help and support in all aspects of the book; to LaUna Huffines for her love, support and encouragement, and for her wonderful ideas for the Playsheets and Introduction; and to Ed and Amerinda Alpern for opening their home and hearts to Orin.

My gratitude to Rob for his faith in me and constant encouragement. I want also to thank my bothers and sisters, David, Robert, Debra, and Patricia; and my nieces and nephews, John, Elise, Mary, Tabatha, Justin, and Heather. I want to thank my mother and father, Shirley and Court Smith, for encouraging and supporting me in my life's work.

I want to thank my editor, Elaine Ratner, who was a delight to work with and whose excellent ideas assisted throughout; Lois Landau for her typing and office help; and Denise Laws for her patient transcription of Orin's channelings.

I want to thank Hal and Linda Kramer for their support and enthusiasm, and for making this book a reality.

I want to thank those who were present during many of these channelings and helped hold a vision of Orin's work: Rob and Stacey Friedman, Nancy and Sara McJunkin, Wendy Grace, Richard Ryal, Scott Catamas, Karen La Puma, Linda Johnston, M.D., Jeff Abbott, Cheryl Williams, Lisa Shara, Lisa Perry, Phyllis Rooney, Adella Pickering-Austin, Paulette St. Martin, Mary Beth Braun, Sandy Chapin, Sallie Deutscher, Sandy Hobson, Leah Warren, Colleen Hicks, Lisa Benson, Linda Nielsen, Mary Pat Mahan, Trudie London, Rosemary Crane, Loretta Ferrier, and Jessica Beckman.

I want to thank those in Dallas who have been so wonderfully supportive of Orin's work: Jean St. Martin, Laurie Schmidt, George and Sandra Pabich, Mark and Patty Dietz, Joan Wall, Philip Huffines, Donald Huffines, Mary Jo Thornton, Deborah DeBerry, M.E. Grundman, Elizabeth Prince, and Elaine Vopni.

I also wish to thank Evelyn Taylor, Cindy Flaherty, and Sebsebie Alemayehu, Shirley Runco, and Diana Peart for encouraging me in the very beginning. I appreciate all the enthusiasm Evelyn poured into being present, assisting, recording, and typing Orin's channelings.

A very special thanks to the bookstores that carry New Age books for helping to awaken people to their higher potential through this wonderful service, and for their support of Orin's work.

CONTENTS

Living
with Joy

To Our Readers

The books we publish are our contribution to an emerging world based on cooperation rather than on competition, on affirmation of the human spirit rather than on self-doubt, and on the certainty that all humanity is connected. Our goal is to touch as many lives as possible with a message of hope for a better world.

Hal and Linda Kramer, Publishers

INTRODUCTION

Many great artists, writers, businessmen, athletes and musicians have reported that their greatest works, inventions and inspiration seemed to be "given" to them from a source beyond their ordinary reality. Scientists often receive their insights and breakthroughs not while working at a desk studying equations, but while in a state of relaxation—perhaps taking a shower, walking on the beach, daydreaming, etc.

This book, *Living with Joy* was "given" to me by a source of wisdom I call Orin while I was in a state of peace and expanded awareness. I received this information in a series of meditation sessions over a period of months. My state of peace was like what we all know in those moments of connection to our higher selves, looking at a beautiful sunset, perhaps in prayer, or holding a young child in our arms. All of us have had moments in our lives, particularly in crisis, when we have suddenly become aware of answers or solutions that were invisible to us before. All of us have experienced times in which we acted beyond our ordinary level of wisdom, strength or courage. Some people attribute those moments of expanded awareness to their higher selves, others attribute it to spiritual guidance.

Those moments of inspiration have been called channeling by some, the gift of prophesy by others, and a connection with the universal mind by others. I call my source of spiritual guidance Orin. I experience him as a loving, wise and gentle master teacher, always positive and compassionate.

Orin and I encourage you to read this book for the wisdom it contains, not because of any claims made about its source. Find within it that which resonates with the truth in you. I have served by being as transparent as possible in order to allow this wisdom to flow through me without taking on my beliefs or coloring the information with my thoughts.

This book can assist you in freeing your heart and expanding into that greater potential that is your birthright. It is a book for those who value new ideas according to the light that those ideas add to their lives. For those of you who want to read more about Orin and how I began channeling, read "Orin's First Appearance" and "Greetings from Orin" which follow on pages one through sixteen. If you wish to jump right into the text, start with "You *Can* Live Joyfully" on page seventeen.

With this book, I invite you to lift up your spirit and join with me in choosing joy, releasing struggle in your life and opening to your potential for personal power and spiritual transformation.

Sanaya Roman

every book I could find on time and space and probable realities, particularly those that explored higher ways of living together as a society, such as *2150* by Thea Alexander. I used to dream that I had a special machine, a time and space machine in which I could visit other planets and lifeforms, go backwards and forward in time, and discover probable realities in which mankind had explored different options for itself. But mostly I wanted to explore the inner realm of the psyche and make my journeys and adventures not to other countries but to other realities. One of the greatest joys of channeling a guide has been the discovery that I have the machine I fantasized about—it is my own mind and a connection with a higher source of light (Orin) that makes possible these various journeys.

I can vividly recall my first real channeling experience when I was seventeen. I had been playing the piano for several hours, feeling very peaceful, and went to lie down by the bay window and watch the stars. All of a sudden, it seemed like I was being talked to inside my head. A "voice" began showing me the earth, explaining that the earth would go through shifts and changes in the future, and that there was nothing to fear. Although I was living in Oregon at the time, the voice said that within a year I would move with my family to California where I would live, but my family would be returning to Oregon. I had spent my childhood moving frequently, living in Kansas, Michigan, California, Missouri and Oregon, so I didn't want to move and didn't like the message. I didn't record what else was said, although it went on for a long time. As it turned out, six months later my dad unexpectedly began a business in San Francisco, and moved the family there. By then, I was going to college in Oregon and was sure I wouldn't come to California with my family. However, one year later, the University of Oregon decided to charge me out-of-state tuition, so I transferred to the University of California in Berkeley and moved to the San Francisco Bay Area. My parents would move back to Portland eight years later.

About the time I was twenty-six I became good friends with a woman named Evelyn Taylor. She came over one day with a Ouija board, saying she knew we could bring through a guide. (I had, as a child of eight or nine, gotten many messages from the Ouija board, playing on it with my great aunt in Kansas. At that age, I recall feeling I was "cheating" because the messages often came into my mind before my fingers.) Cindy Flaherty, another friend, was reading the first Seth book, *The Coming of Seth*, as well as *Seth Speaks*, and we spent many excited hours discussing them.

We began getting messages right away. I spent many evenings on the Ouija board with Cindy and Eve, meeting three or more nights a week, and often friends would join us. It was obvious from the beginning that the messages were coming through me, so Cindy and Eve took turns, one working with me while the other wrote down, letter by letter, all the messages. We accumulated more than 200 pages of notes that first year.

We asked for the highest possible guide and teacher to come to us and shortly thereafter, on October 9, 1977, Orin appeared.

"Who's there?" we asked, when it became apparent that another entity was on the board.

Orin.

"What is your status?"

I am Master Life, above all so far. Your progress is sufficient to receive me now. Your messages will be delivered clearly. Time to start with your progress and learning. I am going to start making assignments. Meditation everyday essential, upon rising and retiring.

After several months, I felt a strong inner urge to speak the messages I was getting on the Ouija board, but didn't know how to start. I sensed whole realms of ideas behind every painstakingly spelled out word but I didn't feel confident enough to speak, and I was afraid that I couldn't do it.

Events soon conspired to get me moving, however. I was driving home in my Volkswagon Bug when a car suddenly pulled out in front of me, causing me to slam on my brakes. The brakes locked, and the car started swerving, out of control, on a four-lane freeway. I was headed for the guardrail and a drop of several stories. Something happened at that moment, a feeling beyond description. It was as if I expanded in time and space, able to check out the future and see myself living. I had an instant awareness of every other driver on the road and felt them as one cohesive unit, with everyone aware and assisting me at a real and energy level. Suddenly the car began rolling over, and I had a glimpse of myself as existing in other dimensions—like a door opening into other realities. The car landed right side up. Other than a bad bruise I was fine. As I looked back on the freeway, I could see that every car had stopped, matching my vision that everyone was working together. I felt different all day, and that night I knew when we met for the Ouija board session I would start channeling.

Everyone sat expectantly as I began. We put away the board, and I sat on a chair with my eyes closed. At first the message I received was like listening to a tape recorder going too fast—ideas would zoom across my awareness before I could speak them. I asked for the words to come more slowly, and then they came so slowly my mind would wander and I would lose the connection. I did bring through coherent and meaningful messages, however, and the evening was an exciting success. I spoke with my own voice, for I was very shy about appearing strange or different to my friends. I would suppress the gestures and the voice that I knew were a part of the being, Dan, who was speaking through me. Orin later explained that Dan would represent him until I could handle Orin's powerful vibration and thought-impulses.

Channeling required tremendous concentration. It was like finding a station on TV, one that you could only bring in as long as you held the thought of it steady and unwavering. After a while, I was able to feel my own thoughts alongside Dan's. I would ask him questions mentally while he was explaining something to someone, and I could feel his reply to me even while I was channeling a message from him to someone else.

The next three years were spent doing many, many readings. In retrospect, I realize it was a time of practice, practice, practice. All the messages were extremely loving, and came from Dan. Orin could only come through on the Ouija board, as was apparent when I tried to let him come through me and almost passed out. At first I felt like I was expanding from top to bottom, becoming spongelike, larger than the room, but still encased in an energy field. I felt a crushing sensation in my chest, and a sense of power and love. My

perception of light and color changed. I was so over-
whelmed with these feelings that I stopped trying to
bring in Orin through my voice. His message to us on
the Ouija board at that time was:

> *I give light, love, and respect to those who come,
> as well as information. I am indeed full of energy
> and it is I who is Dan's overseer and guide. He
> receives from me much like you receive from him. I
> have much energy at a different frequency than
> Dan, and much power in my being. I am sending
> energy to you through the being of Dan, who steps
> down my energy to a level you can manage. Your
> body is like an electrical wire that can only handle
> 20 watts—and I am more like 50 watts!*

In the summer of 1981, I had an urge to buy a very
good tape recorder. After I bought it, I rushed home to
plug it in and try it out. I remember sitting in a chair
with the microphones ready and the tape recorder
loaded with a blank tape. The next thing I knew I was
coming out of a very heavy, almost dreamlike trance
state, discovering I had made a tape. I played it back
excitedly, and realized I had just channeled Orin for the
first time with my voice. It was a guided meditation
that relaxed my body and talked directly to my subconscious to open my channel to him. I listened to it every
day. Orin suggested that I practice channeling at a
slower rate, until I found the right rhythm. He in-
structed me on breathing, and suggested that I take up
aerobic exercise and get out in nature more often. I
could bring him through without all the changes he
was encouraging me to make in my body, but he was

concerned that his higher vibration and frequency not cause my body to prematurely burn out.

I began to know Orin as I channeled the tapes. I was able to hold his energy for 20 or 30 minutes, the length of the meditations. I asked Orin to make a tape for me on every topic I could think of. When I wanted to feel more powerful, gain clarity, achieve certain goals, let go of pain or fear, or feel inner peace, I asked for a tape. Orin told me that one of the fastest and most effective ways to change anything was to work directly with the subconscious, putting in new ideas and releasing old ones. The tapes put new, higher thoughts into my subconscious which would automatically create the changes I was asking for. I channeled many tapes, and friends began asking for copies as they also wanted to experience the positive changes that were happening to me.

Once I was able to bring Orin through verbally, Dan slowly left until one day he bid us all goodbye, saying that as I became attuned to Orin it was difficult for him to come through, and that his purpose has been accomplished. From then on, Orin was my guide, giving readings, teaching people, and assisting me with my spiritual development.

I experienced Orin as a very wise, loving being. Occasionally he would talk directly to me, either through my voice or into my mind, helping me in so many ways. He had a way of looking at the world that was definitely different from mine. There was no coercion on his part; I did not have to see the world his way. But things worked better and I felt better when I used his wiser, more compassionate and much more loving perspective. I started looking at people and events, wondering how Orin would interpret them. Life began to feel better, and I felt peaceful and joyful more frequently. Orin was directing my consciousness to a higher level where I could function more effectivelv in both my inner and outer worlds, aligning them for purpose, direction and a sense of well-being.

In April of 1983, Orin began telling me about a book he wanted to create:

> *I am developing a philosophy and helping plant a new mass thoughtform on earth, one that will help people find their power, reach their hearts and create more happiness and peace in their lives. I want to assist everyone who is ready to receive their higher good and live in higher purpose. We will be helping people understand their minds and emotions, and evolve to a higher consciousness. I want to assist people in discovering that they may create peace and joy, and believe in themselves as loving beings.*

Orin's readings have always reflected this philosophy. When someone comes to him for advice, he is always loving; he gives people a new, more expansive view of their lives and purpose. He has pointed out beliefs that were in conflict, causing pain or frustration, and has given practical, stimulating exercises to bring in new beliefs. He always encourages people to use their own discrimination, to use the information that fits and to let go of anything that does not fit their experience. He never tells people what to do, although if they ask he shows them their choices. He helps them discover what is important in their lives so that their decisions will be reflections of their souls and not their personalities.

Orin is aware of every soul that reaches him through his words, either spoken or written. His light is always available to those who have made contact with him, holding within their minds the thought of light and love that is Orin. In his words is a recognition of who you are—a being of light and perfection experiencing the world of earth, evolving and growing and learning how to express your soul's light in the world of form and matter.

Orin made it clear from the beginning he is here to help heal the healers and teach the teachers. He is drawing to him those who want to be involved in the forefront of a new movement, one that will open more people to their higher selves.

This book, then, is Orin's gift.

II

Greetings
From Orin

Greetings from Orin to you who are here to learn about the higher levels of knowledge. Once these levels are mastered, daily living becomes simpler and the challenge then becomes one of reaching even higher levels and staying there. You will be spending this time as visitors who will later become residents in these realms of knowledge. I am taking all of you there so that you may pass on the information, for you who are apprentices now will be the teachers later, having your own students in time. The wiser and more compassionate you become the more others will naturally seek out your counsel and advice. I speak to you to assist you in reaching a new, more expanded state of awareness and being that will enable you to be among the leaders of the new age. For there will always be those who go out in advance, the scouts and the pioneers—those that dare to go first.

The challenge I offer all of you is to be first into these new levels of consciousness and awareness. For this wisdom, once you read and assimilate it, will seem as if you have known it all along. Anything you learn you may find yourself giving to others, as well as using for your own understanding and guidance. I am calling to any who are here on the earth plane as teachers and healers, to any who wish to be first to step out of the common mass of thinking, to any who are ready to go beyond this known reality and enter into other realms of light and love.

I will assist you in reaching your soul and its greater awareness, and help you discover the joy that awaits you as you look through the windows of your soul. Joy is an attitude; it is the presence of love—for self and others. It comes from a feeling of inner peace, the ability to give and receive, and appreciation of the self and others. It is a state of gratitude and compassion, a feeling of connection to your higher self.

In this book, you will learn how to create a nurturing, supportive environment in which your spirit can unfold. I will attempt to help you recognize your path and higher purpose, and show you how to open to it. This book is dedicated to helping you see who you really are, to showing you how to step onto the path of joy and light. The tools it contains can enable you to live a life of ease, and yet I laugh lovingly as I say ease. For those situations you consider difficult right now you will soon handle with grace, but the new challenges that come will be magnificent. This is a course in exploring your higher self.

There are many states of awareness that you experience but do not pay attention to. You can learn to become aware of higher levels of information and consciousness by focusing on them. You can experience knowledge and true wisdom. I will assist you in exploring and expanding your ability to listen to your soul's guidance. You will learn to tap into whatever information the universe has that will assist you. Each of you who is called to this book can be a channel of healing and love. Each of you is on the path of planetary service and accelerated personal evolution. You express it in many different ways, such as healing through your hands, sharing knowledge through speaking or writing, entertaining others, and spreading light and love to those around you.

Many realities exist and I would like to lead you into some of the higher and finer realms of love, joy and wisdom. I ask you, as you read this, to reach out and stretch your thinking into new ideas that right now may not be accepted by the masses. As human consciousness expands, there will be more and more people reaching these new levels of love. These concepts will be the norm one hundred years from now.

You *are seeding the world with new thoughtforms.*

I extend an invitation to anyone who is willing to be a part of the change that is coming. Many such as I are calling you together. Imagine yourself as part of a larger group, all coming together to explore consciousness, to seed the universe with the new ideas that are coming. These ideas are beliefs that the universe is friendly, that it is abundant, and that you *can* live in a state of joy and love. As you contribute your higher thoughts to the "general atmosphere," you are creating ideas that will assist others in loving themselves more.

I am inviting those of you on a path of light and joy to join with my essence as you read these pages, and feel the community of all who are sharing this knowledge. There is much that can be accomplished by a group holding certain thoughtforms in their joint mind. Whenever certain thoughts and beliefs are held and practiced by a group of people—and the focus here is love, spiritual growth and higher purpose—they magnify tenfold the ability of each person to create them in his life, and make those thoughts available to others who are reaching upward.

Your country and the world are already undergoing transformation. In the next twenty years there will be major changes in the mass thoughtforms. You can help plant the thoughts that are to come. You can hold within you an image of greatness, of universal concerns, and of helping the earth itself. To utilize the energy and changes that are coming, you will need to develop such soul qualities as peace, clarity, love and joy. I am not speaking of a holocaust that is coming, for I do not see that happening. I am speaking of the need to bring peace to the planet by bringing it into your own life. It is an opportunity for you to utilize the energy and transitional atmosphere of your times to propel yourself into a higher consciousness.

There are many wise teachers and we are all bringing through the same message of universal love, peace and oneness. We speak in different vocabularies, using the words that best reach the groups we are with. It has begun in many places. You have probably felt a sense of community with all those who are focusing on expanded awareness and self-growth. You may find yourself in two worlds, connecting with people who do not believe in these things and those who do. You may discover that you have relationships that span several worlds, for this information must not be planted in just one place. We are seeking people who will cross-pollinate the world, who are willing to be a part of more than their own group of like-minded people. The more areas you can be a part of, the more valuable you and your ideas will be to the planet.

You can learn ways to transcend power struggles and move your relationships into the heart and soul, connecting with each other in a more loving way. You will be learning many joyful ways to link with your friends and others in your life, to establish connections that will bring you joy and inner peace. Those who read this are on a path of uniting with other people from the heart and not from the power center. What you learn can be passed on and shared. It is time for new thoughtforms on the planet, new ways of joining and being with each other, ways that create peace and not disharmony.

Who am I?

So many of you have asked what is a guide? Who are we? What is our purpose? I, Orin, am a spiritual teacher. I can exist in other systems of reality besides those that are based on your scientific principles and laws. I have experienced a lifetime on this planet so I could know better the experience of physical reality.

I travel into many systems. In your world, you might call me a researcher, reporter, teacher and guide, but that is only a part of who I am. I connect with many planes of reality, for right now on an interplanetary scale there is great growth and evolution occurring in all kingdoms. In the worlds I travel to, growth is accelerating. Help is being given at all levels to those who ask. I am in spirit right now and I speak to the spirit of the one you call Sanaya through the transmission of my thought-impulses.

I am a Being of Light.

I am assisting you who are on a path of light and joy on earth, who are willing to serve the planet and are interested in personal growth and evolution. I offer guidance and assistance in both your personal life and your path of world service.

I am transmitting spiritual teachings to the earth plane and also many others. I travel to various parts of the universe to discover what is happening, and assist in focusing and directing guidance to those areas that can benefit from it the most. There are certain truths which operate throughout the known universes; I am here to teach those principles and practices. The understanding and practice of these truths always creates expanded awareness and growth.

I invite your soul to join with me as we explore your greater potential. My essence is in these thoughts and will help you open to your deeper, wiser self. It will feel as if you are becoming who you always knew you were. Many of you have always felt different from those around, as if you knew you had a mission, something special to accomplish with your life. I hope to help you discover that mission and purpose. I invite you to journey with me to the realms of light and love you come from.

Many of you beautiful souls of light have gotten caught in the denser energies of the earth. With these concepts I will attempt to lead you back to those finer realms you so naturally seek. Allow yourself to absorb the energy behind the words for this is written in such a way that both the words and the energy I send with them will open your heart.

*There is great love,
compassion, and guidance
available through us,
the Beings of Light.*

I am not distant, and my love, my vibration reaches out to any who ask for it. You must ask however, before anything can be given you, for we cannot help those who do not ask.

This is the beginning of the course. What I am saying is but a small part of what will be happening to all of you. I hope that in some way I can make the transition of the next years joyful, for all of you are undergoing major change. I encourage you to accept into your heart only those ideas and suggestions that ring true to the deepest part of your being, and let go of any that do not. I am here as an assistant, a spiritual teacher, to help you with your own personal transformation. I welcome you to a more joyful, loving and peaceful vision of who you are.

III

You Can Live Joyfully

I will speak of joy, compassion and higher purpose, for many of you are searching for peace and a sense of inner completion. Most of you are aware that peace comes from your inner world, and that the outer world is a symbolic representation of that which is within. You are all at different levels of perceiving the process by which you create what you experience.

What is the path of joy? There are many life-paths you can choose, just as there are many ways you can serve on a planetary level. There is a path of will, a path of struggle, and also a path of joy and compassion.

*Joy is an inner note
that you sound
as you move through
the day.*

What brings joy into your life? Do you know? Are you aware of that which makes you happy? Or are you so busy fulfilling your daily obligations that you put off to some future time those things that make you feel good? The path of joy deals with present and not future time. Are you holding an image of what life *will be* like some day when you are happy, but not feeling that sense of well-being right now, today?

Many of you fill your time with activities that are not soul directed, but activities of the personality. You may have been taught that being busy creates self-worth. There are two kinds of busyness, however. Personality-directed activity is often based on "shoulds" and is not done to benefit your higher purpose, while soul-directed activity is always done with your higher purpose in mind.

The personality is often distracted by the senses, which capture its attention from moment to moment. The phone call, the child, the constant voices, the emotions of others—all are energies that grab your attention throughout the day, and can distract you from your inner-directed messages.

True joy comes from operating with Inner-Directedness and recognizing who you are.

You may have many reasons why you cannot change your life right now. If you do not begin to create reasons why you can, change will always be a future thought, and you will not be on the path of joy. In this world you have chosen to come into, you have been given physical senses and an emotional body. Your great challenge is not to be distracted by that which comes in front of you, or that which is pulling on you or calling to you, but instead to find your center and magnetize to yourself all those things that are in alignment with your inner being.

Are you setting it up so that people are pulling on you, so that your time is full, but is not filled with the things you want? You have the power to change that drama. It comes from your compassion for who you are, and from your sense of inner freedom.

Many of you have set up lives for yourselves that are not joyful because you believe that you are obligated to others, that you need to be needed, or that you are enslaved by one situation or another.

The *challenge of the path of joy is to create freedom.*

Every person is free. You may have created an arena of work, and based your life upon certain accomplishments and forms. The path of joy is learning not to be caught by the details of those forms. It is learning not to be trapped by your own creations, but to be uplifted by them.

If you have created a job, a relationship, or anything that is not bringing you joy, look inward and ask why you feel you must be in a relationship with anything or anyone that does not bring you joy. Often it is because you do not believe you deserve to have what you want. There is no such thing as "deserving" on our plane. You have all been given active imaginations; they are your doorways out of where you are. Yours can be a doorway into worry, if that is how you use it, or it can be a doorway into joy.

As you are on the phone during the day, speaking to your friends, do you let them talk on long past when you would like them to be gone? Do you listen to their stories that bring down your energy? Do you make appointments to see people, even though you do not truly have the time, or when there is no higher purpose in being with them? To find the path of joy you will want to ask why you feel obligated to people or to the forms you have created.

The path of compassion does not obligate you to love everyone regardless of how they act or who they are. It is a path of seeing the truth of who they are, acknowledging all their parts. It is the path of looking at people and asking is there anything you can do to heal, assist, or bring them in touch with their higher vision? If there is not, then you are pulling down your own energy by spending time with them.

Some of you are helping people over and over, feeling frustrated. You may feel obligated, as if there were no way out except to listen to their tales of woe, wishing that they would get on with their lives. If you are helping people and they are not growing, then you had better look again to see if you are indeed helping them, or if they are capable of receiving the help you are giving.

The path of joy involves the ability to receive. You can be surrounded with love, friends that care, and have a healthy and fit body, if you choose. There is so much to be grateful for and appreciate. One of the ways to receive more is to spend time appreciating what you have. Acknowledge even the simplest things—the flowers you drive by, the heartwarming smile of a child, and you will soon find the universe sending you even more.

For those of you who are concerned about money or finding a career where you can make money doing what you love, have you been willing to take a risk and do what you love? Have you been willing to trust the universe to give the opportunity to you? And even more, are you prepared to handle the money when it comes? Do you feel you deserve it?

The path of joy involves valuing yourself and monitoring where you put your time.

If every single person spent time only where he accomplished the greatest good for himself and the person he was with, the world would change in a day. It is important to spend time in ways that promote your highest good. If something is not for your highest good, I can guarantee that it is not for the highest good of the planet or others either.

You may ask, what am I here to do that will bring me joy? Each one of you has things that you love to do. There is not one person alive who does not have something he loves to do.

What you love is a sign from your higher self of what you are to do.

You may say, I love to read and meditate; certainly that can't be my path and bring me money. However, if you allowed yourself to sit and read and meditate, a path would unfold. So often you resist what you most want to do. In everyone's mind there is a whisper of the next step. It may be simple, such as making a phone call, or reading a book. It may be a very concrete, mundane thing to do that may not even seem connected with your higher vision. Know that you are always being shown the next step; it is always something that comes to your mind as an obvious, simple and joyful thing to do.

You all know what would bring you joy tomorrow. When you wake up, ask yourself what you could do with the day that would bring you joy and delight. Put a smile on your face, rather than focusing on how you are going to get through another day. Don't focus on the problems you have to handle.

*You will have joy only when
you focus on having it and
settle for nothing less.*

What is your highest vision and how do you find it in your life? Most of you have many distractions that need not be. If you were to sit for even five minutes each day, reviewing what you set up for the day, and ask how each appointment, person or phone call fits into your higher purpose, in a few short months you would be on the path of your destiny and would discover ways to double your income. Of course, you will need to *act* upon this wisdom.

If you do not know what your path is, you can create a symbol for it. Imagine that you are holding it in your hands as a ball of light. Bring it up to your heart, then into your crown chakra at the top of your head, and release it to your soul. Very shortly, it will begin to take form. You will find that at just the thought of higher purpose you will begin to magically and magnetically rearrange your day. Suddenly friends who took your time will no longer look so interesting, as you bring in new friends and change the nature of your friendships with old acquaintances.

Compassion is caring for yourself; valuing yourself and your time. You do not owe anyone your time. When you take charge of yourself and affirm that you are a unique and valuable person, the world will affirm it to you also.

E*very person has a purpose and a reason for being on earth.*

There is not just one thing you are here to do, for each thing you accomplish becomes part of an earlier step and another stage of your evolution. Each experience is integrated into earlier experiences. Some of you step sideways, trying out new and seemingly unrelated things, to bring in new skills on the journey upwards. Some of you find form for your work. Some of you are here to develop, as your purpose, a vision of peace within.

Do not judge purpose by the standards of others, or by what society has told you is the best thing to do. You may be here to develop inner peace and radiate that quality outward, making it available to others. You may be here to explore the realm of the intellect or the business world, to assist the thoughtforms on the planet at that level. Compassion is outside of judgment. It is simple acceptance, the ability to love and to value the self, and whatever path of higher purpose unfolds.

There is tension worldwide at almost all times, but there is also great opportunity available for those who are focused on the positive, and willing to take responsibility for everything they create. Energy is available to those who are intuitive and healing and on a path of joy. With that energy comes an opportunity to have great abundance and joy *now*.

Many of you are moving ahead rapidly. You have been on an accelerated path of growth so that you may heal and teach others who are following. Some of you, such as authors and writers, may be years ahead of the mass thoughtforms, as it is necessary for you to be in the flow of the times when your writing comes out. Not everyone is experiencing the same transition at the same time.

All of you reading this are pioneers, for you would not be attracted to this information if you were not ahead of your time.

You may be feeling a change in the energy of the planet. Those of you who are willing to look upward and find your vision will find your lives even more accelerated. If you think you are busy right now—be prepared! Things will happen even faster, and that is why wisdom and discernment are becoming increasingly important. That is why you will want to look at each day and compare it to your higher purpose.

Sometimes the hardest thing of all is saying "no" to someone in need. If you constantly pay attention to people in crisis, you affirm that the way for them to get your attention is by creating crisis. If you want people in your life to respect and honor your time, teach them by rewarding them when they do so.

The world is going through a change, things are speeding up. You may already be feeling it. Those who are not focused on their higher vision and self will experience even more problems. Some of the people around you may be speaking of this as the greatest, most joyful time of their lives, while others are speaking of it as the most difficult. If you are experiencing this as the most joyful time in your life, look around at others. Rather than judging or feeling separate from those who are having difficulties, simply send them light, and then let go.

If you find yourself in power struggles with people— strangers, loved ones or close friends—go into your higher self. Stop for a moment, take a deep breath, and don't get caught in their desire for a confrontation. Remember, it's their desire, *not* yours.

In this accelerated vibration of the planet, you will want to learn not to be pulled into other people's energy through the third chakra, the solar plexus. Much of the energy that people experience from others comes through the solar plexus, the power and emotional center. Many of your challenges on the path of joy will be to step outside of power struggles and come from a deep level of compassion. If a friend snaps at you or is unfriendly, step back, and with a sense of compassion, try to experience life from his perspective. You may see his tiredness, or his defensiveness, which has nothing to do with you, for you only represent another character in his play. The more you can step outside and not be pulled into power struggles, the more peaceful and abundant your life will be, and the more you will be in a position to heal others by being in your heart with compassion.

Go inward for a moment and ask yourself what you can do tomorrow, specifically, to bring more joy into your life. Ask what you can do to let go of a power struggle or an issue that is going on in your life and draining your energy. What can you do tomorrow to free up a little more time to find inner peace?

You have so much to be grateful for, your excellent mind and your unlimited potential. You have the ability to create anything you want; the only limits are those you create for yourself. Wake up in the morning and affirm your freedom. Hold up your higher vision and live the most joyful life you can imagine.

PLAYSHEET

1 | List seven things you love to do, that feel joyful
when you do them, that you haven't done in the
last several months. They may be anything—lying
in the sun, taking a trip, getting a massage, accomplishing a goal, exercising, reading a book.

2 | Beside each of these seven things, list what stops
you from doing it—something either inside (such
as your feelings) or outside (someone or something, such as lack of money, that keeps you from
it).

3 | Take two or three things on your list that hold the most joy for you, and think of one step you can take toward each to bring it into your life.

4 | Mark your calendar with a date and a time that you will bring each of these joyful activities into your life.

IV

Changing the Negative into the Positive

The ability to see all situations, people and events from a positive perspective will help you to rise out of the mass thoughtforms and the denser levels of energy, onto your path of joy. You can bring to those you associate with the belief that everything happens for their good. It is common to hear people complain, speak of being victims, or go on and on about the negative things that have happened to them. Most speaking and communication—on TV, in conversations in restaurants, buses and public places—centers around what is wrong and bad. A way of thinking and relating to others has developed that has strong overtones of righteousness, of right and wrong, and the emphasis is usually on what is wrong. This has at its root your system of polarities, where something is either good or bad, positive or negative, up or down. Changing nega-

tives into positives is part of the propagation of the belief in higher good.

Because you exist in a system of polarities I cannot
speak in a meaningful way without using that framework, so I will use that system in communicating to
you. You can take on the responsibility of educating
those you come in contact with about the positive reasons why things are happening to them.

*If you wish to be aware of the higher
good happening in your own life,
be willing to let go of a limited
perspective and enlarge your
view of your life.*

In many ways your past acts as an anchor until you
release and let go of any negative beliefs about it or
memories of it. Some of you have relationships from
the past you feel you did not handle in the best way
you could. Maybe there is an old hurt in your heart or a
feeling of being let down. You can go back and change
negative memories by looking at the gifts people had
for you and seeing the good you did for them. You then
can telepathically transmit forgiveness and love to those
people at whatever age they were when you knew
them. You will heal yourself and others by doing this.
The healing will occur in present time also, and erase
any projection of negative patterns into your future.

I will start by speaking of the past, for many of you
hold negative images about your past selves. Every day
you are growing and evolving and learning new ways to

handle your energy, and yet, if it had not been for those incidents in the past you would not be who you are now.

Everything that happens is meant to help move you into your greater self.

Now that you have reached a new level of being, you may be tempted to look back at the past with regret. You may think of many higher, more loving ways you could have handled some things. Yet those very incidents provided you with the growth that allows you now to see a better way of behaving. Some lessons may be more painful than others, depending upon how willing you are to face them. When I speak of enlarging your scope of vision I am speaking of being able to step outside of present time and see your life as a whole rather than as a series of unconnected events.

When I, as Orin, view a person, I stand above his or her entire life and look at each incident not as a separate event, but as a part of an entire life path. You have the ability to do this also. You may resist or feel unwilling to take the time, and yet, the gifts that await you are great if you are willing to see your life from a larger perspective. To reframe into the positive, the conscious mind will need to see the larger picture. The spiritual body does see the larger picture. You can learn to move into that larger perspective and out of the emotional and mental body. That will assist you in seeing your life positively.

Most people's emotional bodies are much younger than their spiritual or mental bodies, and are the most caught in dense energy. The emotional level of most people in this country is evolving but is still young. It is not being aided in its evolution by the current belief systems of fear and pessimism. It is our intent, through holding a constant focus of peace and love, to contribute optimism and hope to the emotional atmosphere and belief systems of the people.

The newspapers and the mass media often communicate a feeling of doom that pervades the mental images and emotional feeling tones of the nation. As I am speaking of reframing into the positive, I will add there are *good* reasons why this is happening. If you look at the country from a larger perspective you will see you as a race are changing the path you are on because of these fear-based messages. People respond to certain kinds of messages, and most react to the negative ones that are being put out, including those that warn and those that trigger fear. Right now it has been decided by you as a race that fear works more effectively in changing people than hope; and yet, once the tide has been turned it will be time for new communications of hope and optimism.

When you look around at your society, become aware of the way people are speaking, see the ways they are learning about their energy. Broadcast to them your belief that they can experience growth in positive ways. There are some belief systems right now that are undergoing change and I will mention them so you may assist in bringing through these higher systems of reality more rapidly.

One is a belief that growth comes through pain and struggle. This is one you are getting ready to let go of on a mass level. However, there are many who are not yet ready to exist without pain and struggle so they must be allowed to live in that arena until they are willing to move on.

There is a mass belief that the outer world is more important than the inner world and this is undergoing change also. There is a mass belief in scarcity, that there is not enough for everyone. It is one of the underlying beliefs of your civilization and always is a source of competition and power struggles. There is no negative judgment implied here, only an observation that some people learn in certain ways that make life hard for them. You can be in the forefront of the new thought-forms, so I am calling to your attention the mass beliefs you exist in. Once you recognize them, you may choose whether you agree with them and want to live by them or not.

*Are you willing to believe
in ideas of abundance,
of validating the inner world,
and of learning to grow through joy?*

Starting with your own past, think of a time in which something happened you did not understand. Now, as you look back as an adult, as an older, more mature self, you can understand precisely why you drew that incident to you and what you learned from it. You can see as you look back with the larger picture in mind that when you did not get what you thought you wanted, there was a reason for not having it. Perhaps not having it changed your life path. Maybe having it would have held you back in some way, or maybe it was something you wanted from a smaller, less evolved part of you. As you look back with your memories, reviewing past relationships and career paths (even those you are still in but letting go of), see how they served you. What you have now would not be possible without those experiences. You cannot leave something until you love it. The more you hate something the more bound you are to it, and the more you love it the freer you are. So as you love your past, you are free from it.

When you can think of your childhood and your parents and know that they were perfect for the path you are on, you are then free of the effects of your past. You can believe that you chose your parents, relationships, and careers so that you could be where you are now. As you change your negative memories into positive understanding, you can go even faster into your new future.

You can release the past by loving it.

Every time you think of a bad memory that makes you feel sorry for yourself, or bad about how you acted, or makes you see yourself as a victim, or makes you hold a negative picture of yourself, Stop! See what good you created from that experience. It may be that you learned so much from it you never again brought that kind of behavior back into your life. It may be that because of that situation, you changed your path. It may have brought you an important connection or helped develop new qualities and personality traits. You may have served and helped many people in that job. Your parents may have developed your strength, or your inner will, by creating obstacles for you. People who want to develop muscles, for instance, may use weights to push against. Your parents may have acted as a "weight" for you to push against to develop your inner strength. Everything in your past happened for your good. If you could believe that the universe is friendly, that it is always helping you to create your highest good, you could live a life of more peace and security.

Look at your present time existence. If you wish to see the larger picture you can sit and imagine that you are going into the future. If you are facing a new challenge, one for which you have not yet acquired the necessary skills, imagine yourself going into the future and uniting with your future self, drawing to you the knowledge that future self holds. It may not come into your conscious awareness until the moment you need it, but the energy and knowledge your future self can send you can make what you are going through today seem easier. If you are facing decisions or troubles, imagine yourself five years from now looking back at today, viewing the overall picture. Then link with that self of the future, for from that perspective it would be much simpler to know what to do today. You could even imagine you are that future self and talk to your self of today from that future perspective. You could make things up, telling yourself why you are going through what you are experiencing and affirming to your present self the rightness of everything that is happening. Your future self is real and separated from you only by time. It can talk to you and help you know what to do right now, how to get where you want to go even more quickly.

When you imagine your future,
do you not think you will be
the same then as you are now.

You will be more evolved, wiser, expanded; problems that exist now in your life will be solved. Problems create a focus of attention. They are labelled as problems because you do not yet have a solution, nor is that new part of you yet activated or matured that knows how to deal with the situation effectively. Often you create problems to originate new forms of behavior and evolve parts of yourself. You can do that without creating crisis, by paying attention to the whispers of your mind and by spending time imagining yourself in the future. You can draw to you new images of who you want to be, but you will also want to be willing to release the situations and things in your life that do not fit those images.

The emotional body has the most to gain from reframing everything into the positive, for every time you say a negative word to yourself or make yourself wrong, your emotional body changes its vibration and your energy drops. When the vibration becomes lower your magnetism changes and you attract to yourself people and events that amplify this drop in energy. Once you take responsibility and attune your awareness to higher thoughts, creating joyful images in your mind, you can raise the vibration of your emotional body. Then you will want to have the people in your personal life contribute to and share those high feelings. If you find, however, the people you know are constantly depressed or angry or in a negative emotional state, ask yourself what belief you have that says it is good for you to be in that personal environment.

Most of you have habits and patterns in your personal relationships that repeat themselves regardless of who you are with. If you are willing to release those patterns you will find many new ways of deepening the ties between you and others. If you focus on something wrong with another person you can make it even larger. The things that were working in your relationship before will start not working. On the other hand, if you focus on bringing out the good in other people, seeing their beauty and speaking to them of what you love about them, you will find the areas which were giving you problems beginning to resolve themselves, even though you haven't worked directly on finding solutions. The more you focus on problems between you, or on what is wrong with other people, the more you will find relationships going downhill. When people first get together they are so focused on the good in each other it is said that they wear rose-colored glasses. This is a great gift to each other, for as each pays attention to the good in the other they help each other create it.

*Loving people is a commitment
to holding a high vision of them,
even as time and familiarity
take their toll.*

Many of you, when you see something that is different from you in another person, a lover or friend, go into power struggles or competition to deal with it. If, instead, you accept another's world view and know that it is simply different from yours, you will not need to do anything other than love him or her. You do not need to convince people you are right, for that only draws you into power struggles with them. Nor do you need to be convinced that they are right. Being positive does not mean being blind. It means being willing to see the good in others and to turn the focus away from what is wrong (to you) or different.

The more you point out to others all the ways they are bad or wrong, the more insecure you make them, and from that base of insecurity you actually create and enlarge the problems you focus on. You can tell everyone in your life how good they are, and help them recognize how much they are growing. Whenever they complain of a problem or something wrong you can help them see how the situation is helping them, the positive changes it is giving them, and what it is teaching them.

You may be thinking of your job or lack of one as a problem, or wishing you were out of a career or that you could create one. Your higher self is always watching over you. It is always monitoring you to see if your attitudes, if who you are at the personality, emotional and physical level, are developed enough to have what you want. If it sees you are not ready, it will sidetrack you while it evolves those parts of you that need to be developed. You may need certain skills, to meet new people, or change your environment.

Your higher self will guide you in the right direction so that you can make the changes you are asking for, or have what you want.

If you come from the larger perspective, you will understand that what is happening to you right now is preparing you for more. When you catch people complaining this week, simply say to them, "Stop." Learn to use your voice to halt people's energy when they are giving you their complaints. If you listen to people gripe, if you listen to their negativity, you are putting yourself in a position of being affected by their lower energy. You do not need to listen. By stopping people from telling you their stories, particularly if they are not good ones, you assist them in coming out of it. Watch people this week. Do they go on and on about their sad stories? If so, you are connecting with them at the personality level when you could be relating to them in a higher way.

Ask them what they want and where they are going. What higher purpose can they create? Refocus them on the positive and you will be doing the same for your own energy. This week be willing to listen alertly to everyone who comes your way. Listen to conversations in public places. If you notice that they are not positive, tune them out. But first, mentally send people the thought that the level of development they are at now will evolve, and send love to them for who they are.

Notice the TV, newspapers and books you read—do they use positive words? Do they bring up your energy or do they take it down and plant negative images in your mind? You are absolutely free to choose what you read and hear. No one makes you do anything. This week use that freedom and free will to put yourself in the highest, most supportive environment you can create. Observe and watch what level people are coming from. You will see that you have much to offer by helping others into a higher space. Know that you can carry light and bring it to all those people you contact.

PLAYSHEET

1 | Think of someone you have felt critical about lately.
What especially did you feel critical about?

2 | What do you criticize in yourself that is the same or
opposite of what you criticize in this person? For
example, perhaps you criticize a friend for always
being late. You may pride yourself about being on
time, but find on closer examination that you are
very critical of yourself about issues of time.

3 | Think of a time you did the same thing you are criticizing the other person for. For instance, say you are criticizing your friend for not returning money to you. Was there a time that you did not return borrowed money to someone?

4 | Think of a time you felt warm and loving. Get into that feeling. Now think of the person you're criticizing again. How do you feel towards him or her as you view him with this warm and loving feeling? As you see your friend through loving and compassionate eyes, so do you forgive yourself.

5 | Keep that warm and loving feeling. Think of what you have criticized yourself for. Do you feel more warm and loving towards your own behavior?

V

The Art of
Self Love

There are many ways you can love yourself, and everything that happens to you is an opportunity to have a
loving experience. Seen in the right perspective, anything can provide you with an occasion to love yourself.
When things seem to be going against you, they are
only happening to show you blocks to your usable
power. I am sure if I asked you to make a list of things
to do that would be loving to yourself you would be
able to think of many. There may be a part of you that
reminds you that you're not carrying those things out,
and a battle begins. This inner war can be draining and
making yourself wrong is not a right use of energy.

*Loving yourself means
accepting yourself
as you are right now.*

There are no exceptions to the contract; it is an agreement with yourself to appreciate, validate, accept and support who you are at this moment. It means living in present time. Many of you look back into the past with regret, thinking of how you could have handled a situation in a higher way, imagining if only you had done this or that, things would have worked out better. Some of you look into the future to make who you are right now inadequate. The past can assist you if you remember the times in which you succeeded, creating positive memories, and the future can be your friend if you see that in picturing it you are creating a vision of the next step. Do not make yourself wrong because you have not yet achieved it. It is important to love who you are now without reservation.

Loving the self is beyond attachment and detachment. You exist in physical bodies, and each one of you has a focus which you call the "I." You have been given the "I" so you can separate from a greater whole and experience a particular part of beingness. Everything you have experienced up till now is what you were born to learn about. Whether you label it good or bad, it is what composes your being, your uniqueness and purpose. If you could see yourself from my perspective, you would view yourself as a crystal with many facets. Each of you is completely different, a unique combination of energy. Each of you is beautiful, special, and one-of-a-kind, as is each crystal. You reflect light in a unique way, thus your aura varies from those around you. If you could appreciate your uniqueness, see that the path you have chosen is different from anyone else's, it would be easier to detach from others' views and follow your own guidance.

One of the ways to love the self more is to stop comparing yourself to others. Although you are part of a whole, you are also an individual self, with your own path. The group and family belief systems you have taken on as your own can be obstacles to your self-love. "Everybody says it is good to meditate," you may be hearing, and so you feel bad if you don't do so. The challenge of loving the self is to step aside from everything you are told, and ask, "Does this fit me? Does this bring me joy? Do I feel good when I do it?" It is ultimately your own experience that counts.

There is a temptation to make another person or something like a book an authority, and to put outside of yourself the ability to decide what is good for you. There is much benefit in being with teachers, but only so that you may learn to bring in information and growth for yourself. I exist to open doors for you; I do not wish to take your power, but to give it to you. When you are with teachers, any person you have made an authority in your life, even if it is just a friend, question and listen carefully to what he or she is saying. You may be accepting his or her statements as truth, and it is important to ask if what they are saying is true just for them, or is it something that is good for you also?

Loving the self means stepping outside of guilt.

There is tremendous guilt in this society. Many connections between people come from the solar plexus, the power center, from which people try to persuade, convince, control and manipulate each other. Loving the self means stepping outside of this kind of relationship. To do so you will need to let go of guilt.

If you do not play the same ball game as those around you, you may find them feeling threatened. They want you to think and act in certain ways to fit their pictures, so they try to gain power over you through guilt. Often parents know no other way to be in control; they use guilt, anger and the withdrawal of love to dominate their children. When you feel strong and in charge of your life you can come from the heart. When you feel lacking in control you may feel you must manipulate or engage in power struggles to get what you want. You may think you have to make excuses for your behavior or tell white lies to protect other people's feelings.

When you act this way you are not loving to yourself; instead you give your subconscious a message that who you are is not enough or acceptable to other people. If you wish to be free, it is important not to manipulate other people either, but to give them their freedom. At first you may feel as if you have lost a measure of control if you turn over to other people the right to do as they please with their lives. But you will create between you a whole new level of honesty and love that could not occur without your courage and willingness to release control.

You can learn to detach from the reactions of others and from your own emotions if they take you out of a calm, clear center. Loving yourself means asserting yourself with compassion. When you are willing to show others who you are, you open the door for them to expose their real selves also. Judgment stands as an obstacle to self-love. Every time you judge, you separate. When you form opinions about another person, looking at him and saying, for instance, "this person looks like a lazy person, or a failure, or has terrible clothes," you create a message to your subconscious that the world is a place where you had better act in certain ways if you want to be accepted. By rejecting other people through your judgements, you have set up a message in your own subconscious that you are only going to accept yourself under certain conditions. This leads to an inner dialogue of self-criticism. It can also bring back many negative images to you from the outer world, for once you send out these pictures you have created a pathway for them to come back.

Look at the messages you put out to other people. Do you accept them lovingly, without criticizing or putting them down? Do you smile at them? Are you friendly, do you allow them to feel good about themselves, or do you sit without acknowledging them? If you accept them, even just telepathically (that is in your own mind), you assist them in finding their higher selves. You will find other people accepting you more lovingly also.

Your beliefs about reality
create your experience of it.

It can happen in subtle ways. If you think people do not accept you as you are, that you must try hard to please them, then you will draw those kinds of people into your life. You may find that you end up seeing friends at the times they are tired and non-giving. Whatever you believe to be true about friends or any people in your life, you will create that experience of them. If you say, "this man is warm and affectionate towards me," you will create that in the relationship.

To move into a higher sense of self-love, start identifying what you consider to be facts about the way the world works. If you think that the world is cold and uncaring, or that you must try hard for everything you achieve, then that conviction stands between you and self-love. A belief is what you consider a truth about reality. You may say, "it is a fact that if I smile at people they smile back," but this can be a reality for you and not for other people. Indeed, because of this belief you may choose subconsciously to smile only at people who will smile back. If you believe that people never smile back at you, then you will automatically pick people to smile at who never return it.

If you want to experience a world that is caring and supports your images of self-love, begin looking at what you are saying about the world to yourself. You can change your encounters with people and the world by altering what you expect. It has been said "the world may not be just, but it is exact" and this means that what you get is precisely what you expect and believe you will get. If you are in a profession you "know" is hard to make money in, and you say "not many people make money in my field," you will create that as a fact for yourself. You are holding a certain view of reality, and that will be your experience, not only of your career, but of others you meet in that field also. All you need do is alter what you expect to happen and you will experience a different world.

Another quality of self-love is forgiveness. Some of you hang onto old issues, feeling the anger over and over. It is irritation at yourself, perhaps, or at another who let you down. The higher self knows forgiveness. If there is anything you are hanging onto, an anger, a hurt, a negative feeling about another, then you are keeping it in your aura. The person you are mad at is affected, but not as much as you will be. Anything you are carrying in you towards another sits in your aura and acts as a magnet for more of the same. There is most definitely a reason for forgiveness, for it cleanses and heals your aura.

Self-love also involves humility, which is self-expression from the heart and not from the ego. Humility says, "I am open. I am willing to listen. I may not have all the answers." Humility is one of the qualities that will allow you to receive more, for humility implies openness. It does not imply a lack of self-confidence, but a great amount of faith and trust in yourself.

Only those who feel good about who they are can express humility.

Those who act the most arrogant or coldly confident are those who lack the very characteristics they are trying to project. People who love themselves come across as very loving, generous and kind; they express their self-confidence through humility, forgiveness and inclusiveness. If you know people who seem to be very wise and yet put others down, reject friends, make people feel bad about themselves—no matter how high their words or what they teach, you can rest assured they do not love themselves.

Loving the self involves faith and trust and belief in who you are, and a willingness to take action upon it. It is not enough to feel that faith and trust; you need to experience it in your outer world. You are a physical being, and joy comes from seeing around you those things that express your inner beauty—a garden, flowers, trees, your house, the ocean. All of these are the rewards of acting upon and trusting yourself, of following your path and vision with action. The ultimate challenge of self-love is to act upon it, to speak up to people and to create in the world your heaven on earth.

It is not enough just to give and radiate love; loving the self comes from receiving love also. If you are giving love to everyone, but they cannot receive it, then it has no place to go. You do everyone great service by being willing to receive their love.

One of the greatest gifts you can give others is opening to their love for you.

In any male-female relationship, or between two men or two women, the relationship will succeed to the degree to which each can receive the other's love. Even if you are giving 100 percent, if the other person is receiving only 50 percent, then what you give to him is reduced by half. If what he gives back is only 50 percent, and if you can only receive 50 percent of that, then what you get back is 25 percent, and so on. The result is that you experience less and less love from each other. To experience greater love in your life, be willing to receive gifts from others, offerings of love, friendship and support.

If you want to bring your higher self into your life on a daily basis and increase your self-love, take one characteristic of the soul and whenever you have a moment, think about it. Some of these are: peace, appreciation, humility, harmony, joy, gratefulness, health, abundance, freedom, serenity, strength, integrity, respect, dignity, compassion, forgiveness, will, light, creativity, grace, wisdom, and love. By taking these qualities and reflecting or meditating on them, you will magnetize them to your aura, increase them and draw the recognition of them to you from other people. Whatever you think of, so you are. If every day you pick one of the qualities of the higher self, ponder on and identify with it, you will create it as an experience of yourself.

Self-love involves respecting the self and living in higher purpose. When you put value on yourself, your time, love and vision, so will others. Before you see your friends, ask what is the highest purpose you can create together. Have you ever stayed at someone's house really wanting to leave, but hesitating, not wanting to hurt his feelings? If so, you were valuing him more than yourself. You were giving him the telepathic message that he does not have to respect your time or you, and it should be no surprise if he took you for granted after a while. Whenever you value and respect yourself, speaking with truth about who you are and taking appropriate actions, you not only evolve yourself, but you assist others by your example. The inability to say "no" to people reflects a world view that says other people's feelings are more important than yours, their rights are more significant and should be considered first. When you do this you create energy blockages within yourself, backing up resentment, anger and hurt which then sit in your aura and attract more of the same.

Self-love comes from the heart, in being gentle and giving unconditional love. Some people think self-love means acting powerful and using the will in an aggressive way that denies the rights of others. You have seen people who get their way and who do not care about their effect on others. You call them ruthless. Often, in a similar way, you can be aggressive with yourself, one part of you dominating and controlling the other parts.

Sometimes, the will acts as if it were an enemy, trying to force, direct or make you do certain things. It can feel like a parent, standing over you. To make matters worse, you may think that the things it is trying to force you to do are for your highest good. For instance, you may berate yourself constantly for not being more organized, or not starting something you are putting off. You may make huge lists of things to do and then feel bad if they are not done. This is making the will right and your other self wrong, the self that is resisting the direction of the will. In this case, you are using your will against your self. It may be that your higher self has created the resistance to keep you from doing certain things and is directing you to other doorways.

If it is used in conjunction with the heart to help you in following a path you love, your will can assist you to increase your self-love. The will can be a director of focus. When it is linked with what you love to do there is no end to what is possible or to the boundaries you can transcend. Have you noticed that when you loved to do something, say your favorite hobby, you could work for hours on end and could easily say no to distractions? The will is a force like a river that you can flow with or try to swim against. You can use it either to beckon and invite you towards your higher path or to constantly punish yourself for apparent transgressions. Which system motivates you? Is your will helping you increase your self-love by focusing you on your path of higher purpose and creating the intent and motivation for action?

PLAYSHEET

1 | How would you know if you were acting or thinking in a way that is loving to yourself?

2 | How would tomorrow look if everything you did was an act of self-love?

3 | What would your actions look like if you were loving to yourself in the following areas: your physical body, your intimate relationship, your job or career?

4 | What would you do tomorrow if you were loving to yourself in your relationship, job and physical body? List three specific actions you would take for each of these three areas.

VI

Self-Respect, Self-Esteem, and Self-Worth

What is required to feel good about the self is not the same from person to person. What you require for self-esteem is not necessarily what another person requires. It is important to discover what makes you feel worthy, confident and happy about who you are.

Self-respect at the highest levels comes from honoring your soul. This means speaking and acting from a level of integrity and honesty that reflects your higher self. It means standing by what you believe in (you don't, however, have to convince others to believe in it), and acting in a way that reflects your values. Many of you criticize others for not living up to a value system you consider right, but on closer examination you may not be living up to it yourself. You have seen the person who is always telling everyone how they should act but he himself does anything he pleases. Self-respect means acting out your values and what you say you believe in.

Many of you have one set of values you say you believe in, but you act from another set of values. This leads to a lot of internal conflict. For instance, you may believe in monogamy deep inside, and yet the person you are with is asking for an open relationship. You decide to go along because you want to hold on to this partner. You believe in one set of values, but you are living by another, and there will be a lot of conflict and potential pain around this issue.

How can you know if the values you "think" you want to live by are yours? You often cannot know until you try. You might think that a good person gets up early in the morning, yet you always sleep late. Many of you have values you think you should live by but don't. The best thing to do is to try out these values— get up early in the morning for awhile. Often, what you think are your values turn out to be "shoulds" given to you by others, and when you actually live them you find they don't work for you. Ask yourself what you value. What do you think *good* people do? Are you following these values? It is difficult to feel good about yourself if you are living in a way that goes against your underlying values. It is important to examine your values and either live by them or change them.

S*elf-respect means coming from your power, not your weakness.*

When you complain that someone or something is making you sad or angry, ask yourself, "Why am I choosing to experience that feeling or to react in that way?" Blaming others will always take away your power. If you can discover why you are choosing to feel hurt by their actions you will learn much about yourself. Some of you are afraid that if you stand up for yourself, you will lose someone's love. Some people are quite good at convincing you that you are in the wrong when you do stand up for your beliefs. Thank them silently for providing you with the opportunity to become strong, for often strength is developed in the face of opposition. Self-respect means standing by your deepest truth and knowing your innermost feelings. It means making yourself and not another the authority of your feelings.

Some of you live or associate with people who belittle you and make you wrong. You can end up focusing so much on their feelings that you lose track of your own. A woman was married to a man who constantly made her wrong and criticized many of her actions. She became so focused on his feelings that she never asked herself for all the years they were together how *she* felt about the way he treated her. She was always trying hard to please him, trying to anticipate his moods and whims so she would not be made wrong. Yet, everything she tried ended with him being angry at her. She began to feel she had failed or was in some way a bad person. She spent so many hours analyzing his feelings that she lost touch with her own. Many of you try to please people and as you try to please them, focus more on how they feel than how you feel.

Self-worth means paying attention to how you feel. You do not need reasons why you choose to do something. You do not need to prove anything to another person about your worth. Validate your feelings; do not analyze and question them. Do not go over and over them asking, "Do I really have a reason to feel hurt?" Let your feelings be real for you and honor them. Many of you make other people your authorities. When they tell you you are bad, you believe them. When they tell you everything is all your fault, you believe them. I am not suggesting that you ignore what other people say, either, but instead honor what *you* feel about the issue. It is one thing to be open to constructive criticism and another to constantly try to do what others want you to do when you don't want it for yourself. Creating self-esteem and self-worth involves honoring your own feelings and path and direction. It means honoring yourself with your words, actions and behavior.

Self-esteem means believing in yourself, knowing that you did the best you knew how, even though two days later you could see a better way. It involves making yourself right rather than wrong and allowing yourself to feel good about who you are. Some of you try very hard all the time, pushing yourselves, rushing around and feeling that whatever you do, it is not enough. Trying and working hard to get things done is not necessarily the road to joy. Respect yourself by following your inner flow. Rest, play, think, and take time to get silent. Doing those things that nurture you are ways to increase your self-esteem.

How you treat yourself is how others will treat you.

Do not wait for other people to respect you or treat you in a more positive way. They will not until you treat yourself with respect. You do not have to be around people who do not honor you, respect you or treat you well. If you do find yourself around those kinds of people, act with dignity and remember that they are not respecting you because they do not respect themselves. You can telepathically send out a message about how you want to be treated. Others only take advantage of you and take you for granted if you let them.

You do not need to get angry or demand your rights, for that only creates a power struggle between you and others. Keep your heart open. They most likely cannot recognize their own greater selves and so it is not possible for them to honor yours. You do not want your self-esteem to be based upon how others treat you or view you. No matter how good you feel about yourself, there will always be those who do not treat you in a respectful way, for they have not learned how to treat themselves in a loving way. The relationships you have with others can only be as good as the relationships they have with themselves. If they do not know how to love themselves, that sets a limit as to how much they can love you. No matter how hard you try, how many nice things you do, they cannot give you the love you seek. Forgiveness is the key to feeling good about how others are treating you. Then, release any anger you may be feeling, simply let it go and focus on other things.

Some of you feel your parents are responsible for your lack of self-esteem. You cannot blame your parents, as it was your reaction to them that created any lack of confidence. Two children may come from equally abusive or negative parents and one will grow up feeling good about himself and the other will not. You make the decision to feel bad. Rather than feeling sorry for yourself about your childhood or feeling like a victim of your upbringing, realize you chose to put yourself in that situation to learn something that would assist your soul's growth. You may say, "I have a pattern of men abusing me because of my abusive father." You came to earth to learn something about love and if you don't learn it from your father, you will choose men with similar patterns to teach you what you need to learn. For instance, you may have experienced your father as abusive, and then found that you attracted similar types of men until one day you decided you would no longer be treated that way. One of the lessons you came to learn in this lifetime may be to love and honor yourself, so you created situations in which you were challenged to do so. As soon as you decided to do so, the pattern ended.

E*very situation in your life*
is a learning experience
created by your soul
to teach you how to gain
more love and power.

Children respond in different ways to the same upbringing, as you can see when you observe how different brothers and sisters may be even though they have the same parents. Some children respond to the negative energy around them by becoming loving and gentle. Some are so sensitive that they cannot stand feeling the negative energy and shut down the part of them that feels. Some respond by feeling that they must be hard and put on an outer image of invulnerability. Self-esteem comes from being willing to acknowledge who you are and love yourself just as you are right now. It is difficult to change until you accept who you are. When you honor yourself and your feelings, others cannot affect you.

You are a worthy individual, no matter what your past, no what matter your thoughts, no matter who believes in you. You are life itself, growing and expanding and reaching upward. All people are valuable and beautiful and unique. Every experience you have had was meant to teach you more about creating love in your life.

There is a fine line between respecting the self and being selfish. Some of you feel you have every right to get angry at others because they hurt you. Honor the feelings of others, but do so in such a way that you also honor your own feelings. To accomplish this you will want to come from a high level of speaking and thinking. Speaking of your anger, yelling and screaming, only puts you in a power struggle with another person and closes both your hearts. When someone does something you do not like, open your heart before you speak. If you choose to make a statement, offer it as something you feel rather than something someone did. You can say, "I feel hurt," rather than "*you* hurt me." A powerful way to state it is, "I am *choosing* to feel hurt." Every feeling you have you have chosen.

Self-worth is knowing that you are choosing your feelings at every moment.

When you communicate to other people in a way that honors their deeper being, you always feel better about yourself. You may have noticed that when you got something off your chest by expressing anger or hurt, you often felt worse afterwards. At the very least, there was a sense of incompletion. You cannot leave a situation until you have done so with love. Those situations you leave in anger will be there for you to resolve in the future. It may not be with the same person, but you will create another person and a similar situation to allow you to resolve it with peace and love.

It is important to respect others. If you do not feel respected by others, you may have put yourself in that situation to learn how to have compassion and gentleness in *your* treatment of other people. Being sensitive to other people's feelings is different from trying to please them. Be willing to see their needs and desires. Do you speak curtly to others without paying attention to their feelings? Do you speak with annoyance or irritation? Watch the energy you put out to other people, for whatever you put out you will get back. Become more aware of your effect on other people, for the more you respect them, the more you will receive respect. Honor their worth, their time and their values and you will find them honoring yours.

Some people honor other people all the time and feel they do not get back what they give. In this case, often they do not feel they deserve to be treated well and allow people to take them for granted. It is easy to respect yourself when those around are respecting you. The challenge is to respect yourself when those around you do not. First forgive them and then let go of any need for them to validate you. When you need to be validated by others to feel good about yourself, you take away your power.

It feels good when other people believe in you, trust you, and support you. Yet, if you want to be powerful, it is important not to *need* other people to do so as a condition of believing in yourself. The need for constant validation makes other people the authority and not your own deep self. Your truth may not be the same as other people's truth. The only wrong is when you do not honor your truth and when you accept what is true for another even though it is not true for you. Some people believe in reincarnation and some people do not. It may be that their belief in reincarnation makes life more joyful and easier to live. It may be that the belief that there are no other lifetimes makes this one more important and real. Whatever belief you hold, it is important that you honor it and be open to new ways of seeing things if they create more joy in your life. Do not automatically accept something unless it has the ring of truth for you. Honor your truth, believe in and stand up for yourself, but have compassion for other people.

Remember that you count, you are important, and that you have a unique and special contribution to make to the world. Know that you are a special being. Your dreams, fantasies and goals are as important as anyone else's.

PLAYSHEET

1 | Think of a pattern you seem to be experiencing with people over and over. Write it here:

2 | Get quiet, relax and go within. Ask your deeper, wiser self to show you what you are learning from this. How is it teaching you to respect and love yourself more?

3 | What soul qualities are you developing from this situation? For instance, you may be developing the quality of compassion, honesty, speaking your deepest truth, peace, self-love, humility, harmlessness, taking responsibility for your actions, etc.

VII

Refining the Ego—
Recognizing who you are

It is important to recognize who you are, without being too egotistical or too humble. It is the two-fold problem of being all you can be. Many of you have not developed a picture of power that you would want to emulate. Many of your images and role models of powerful people come from those who have abused and misused their influence. Therefore, many of you have held back from using your power, because the images you hold of it are negative.

> **I**t is important to develop
> positive pictures about
> the nature of power.

Many of you are very evolved, have much inner sight and wisdom and are looking for ways to express it in the outer world. Learn to tell the difference between those people who are truly influential and full of light and those who only wear the cloak of power. This skill will assist you on your path of joy for it will also help you to recognize your own nobility. Think now of a person you consider powerful, male or female. What is it about that person that you admire? You all know people who have a great deal of authority and yet, when you are with them you feel depreciated, ignored, or put down. I speak of those people who seem to be in a position of power and control and who have many people around them. I will say that true power is the ability to motivate, love, encourage, and help people recognize who they are.

Think now of people you know who have changed your life. In knowing them you felt inspired and expanded. Think of how they used their influence. It is important to recognize people who are full of light, for they come in many forms and packages. And it is time to be aware of those people who are not leading you to a path of greater light and joy. If you can clearly identify those people who have your greatest good in mind, and surround yourself with them, you will grow more rapidly and have much more to offer others.

Evolved people are very gentle souls. Some evolved souls do not yet recognize who they are, and may be too humble. They are most often generous, helpful, and friendly. It may seem as if they cannot do enough for you. I am talking about a certain level of development where the personality does not yet recognize the level of the soul. Many of you are too humble, still wearing the cloak of self-doubt, of wondering who you are. You who are so kind and loving are full of light; you have so much to offer the world. It is important for you to take off your veil, for it hinders you in serving on a larger scale. When you pay attention to your doubts and fears, to that little voice saying, "You're not good enough," you are simply giving heed to your lower self. You have the ability to change your focus.

$$P_{ay}\ attention\ to\ your\ higher\ nature,$$
$$and\ your\ lower\ one\ will\ simply$$
$$wither\ from\ lack\ of\ attention.$$

You do not need to pay attention to those voices within you that create pain, or make you feel less competent, smart or able. You can simply act as if that part of you were a small child; hold it, reassure it, and move on. Do not let those voices attract too much of your attention, and do not think that you are them either. Learn not to pay attention to the little voices within that would have you think you are not great.

The basic nobility of your soul is seeking expression in your actions. What qualities or personality traits would you like to have? Which character traits do you already have that you feel good about? Realize that the qualities you would like to be, you already have. You are simply looking for an increased expression of them in your life.

There is a fine line between egotistical and humble. Walking that line brings the expression of power into balance. Do you brag about yourself? Do you go around wanting to tell people when you did something great? Or do you listen to people with an open ear, putting your own accomplishments aside? The tendency to overstate or exaggerate accomplishments can create problems. Do you find yourself rehearsing what you are going to say to someone about something wonderful you accomplished? There is a difference between coming from confidence and coming from egotism.

If you feel you have done or are doing something great or unusual, you are sending a message to your subconscious telling it that this is not a normal achievement. If you want to bring more great accomplishments into your life, then take them in stride when they happen. (Congratulate yourself, but let it seem as if it is something you do every day.) For instance, some of you go on diets. When you succeed for one or two days, you tell yourself how wonderfully you did. Thus you tell your subconscious that this is an extraordinary occurrence and not a normal one. If you want to change your nutritional habits and you eat healthy food for a day or two, instead of feeling you have accomplished a great deed, view it as something you do every day. Take it in stride. You will then begin to set up a vision of healthful eating as your normal mode of being. Later however, when it has become an established way of life, do let yourself feel good about the change you have made.

There are times when you need to congratulate yourself far more than you do. This is the other side, not too much egotism but the lack of it. Some of you achieve your goals and never stop to acknowledge or congratulate yourselves; you simply focus on the next thing you must do. You lack awareness of your achievements and give yourselves no acknowledgement for your accomplishments.

It is important to become aware of the attention you pay to who you are not. You may say, "I need to do this or that. Why am I always so unorganized, so unfocused?" Be aware that as you think of your lack of certain qualities, you bring that lack into yourself.

Whatever you pay attention to is what you create.

If you spend time feeling bad about something you did, feeling that you were not powerful, or that you did not say the right thing, or if you focus on the things you are not, you increase their power over you. Instead, recognize the qualities you have. Take the things you want to become, and remember those times when you demonstrated those qualities. The more you see within yourself what you want to become, the more you will become it. If you say to yourself, "I have no will power, I never get things done," then you are simply sending that energy out into the future. If, on the other hand, you begin saying to yourself, "I love the way I act around people; I have so much will power, I am so focused," you will experience a new energy coming up from within. You will find yourself becoming that quality. Every time you have a negative image of yourself, saying things such as "I never get things done, I don't have enough time," you send out an image to the world, broadcast that quality, and create that circumstance in your life. If you say positive things about yourself, you will become them also.

Very enlightened and evolved souls know how to show their greatness and power and not create defensiveness, but devotion. If you want people to respect and look up to you, know that it will not happen because you walk around telling everyone how great you are. You have seen people who do that; they invite attack. You have also seen people who are truly evolved, who smile, who recognize greatness in other people, whose focus is assisting and helping. That is true power. It comes from the inner image you hold of yourself. You do not need to tell people if you are peaceful or focused; they know it. Communication is telepathic.

*The images you send out
about yourself into the world
determine how other people see you.*

If you walk around telling people something about yourself you do not feel is true inside, people will sense it. On the other hand, if you know that you have a particular quality or personality trait, everywhere you go people will recognize it in you and support you for it, even if you do not tell them about it.

A refined ego has the ability to get along with other people, to assist them in seeing their nobility and power. Competition often comes from those who do not see who they are, who do not have basic trust in their inner greatness. It comes from a lack of confidence. When you are truly secure, when you know and experience the abundance available, there is no need to compete. You will instead help others create abundance in their lives, be it money, love or success. You will want to assist others in seeing who they are because you have all you need and recognize who you are.

When you are with your friends, are you concerned about what they think of you? If you want them to respect and look up to you, then spend time listening to them. Help them focus on their higher good; assist them in seeing their beauty and inner light. People who have true power are not concerned with the impression they make. They are more interested in the person they

are with than themselves. They find their sense of inner peace increasing.

> M*any of you have been afraid*
> *to assert your power,*
> *because of your mistaken and*
> *negative images of power.*

There is a need for more role models and leaders who
are examples of positive authority. Many of your great
spiritual leaders have come to show new images of
power, refined power. An influential person is someone
who can direct his will to higher good; that is true
power. Someone who is concerned with assisting and
healing others is demonstrating power. Even if people
speak profound words and talk about wise things, if
you do not feel increased and expanded when you are
with them, as if you have gained access to a deeper
level of your being, then you have not experienced true
power.

If you want the people around you to experience your
power and recognize who you are, listen to them with
your heart and do not worry about the impression you
are making on them. Care about them and attend to
them. Pay attention with your heart, and focus on how
you may raise their consciousness and energy. True
power can be seen in the eyes. There is such love in the
eyes of those who are truly powerful, and they look at
you directly. They do not avoid your eyes, but look
straight into them. You feel they really care about you.
They pay attention to what you are saying. Do you give
that kind of alert awareness to people? Do you pay

attention? Do you look in their eyes when you speak? Do you listen to what they say or are you busy constructing your reply or thinking of a defense? Does your mind frequently wander to other things while they are talking? Pay attention with your heart, listen to the unspoken words, for all of these are ways to develop your power.

Look at those people who are nice and gentle, who cannot do enough for you, or give you enough love. Increase those people in your life; draw them to you. You have heard the expression, "The meek shall inherit the earth." It means that power is expressed through humility. Truly powerful people have great humility. They do not try to impress, they do not try to be influential. They simply are. People are magnetically drawn to them. They are most often very silent and focused, aware of their core selves. They know that everything in the outer universe is simply symbolic of their inner worlds. They are in charge of their destinies, and often have around them many people who seek them out for advice. People feel recharged and regenerated by their contact. They do not try to convince anyone of anything; they only invite and offer. They never persuade, nor do they use manipulation or aggressiveness to get their way. They listen. If there is anything they can offer to assist you, they offer it; if not, they are silent.

In the next week, look around at the role models you have chosen, and redefine power in your life. See it as that gentle flowing river of energy that is directed by the soul. Become aware of who you are. Broadcast to the universe positive, loving images about yourself and watch people respond. Be willing to use your higher qualities and recognize your abilities.

PLAYSHEET

1 | Think of two people you know who have really
made a difference in your life, who have encour-
aged, loved, and motivated you, or left you feeling
inspired and expanded.

2 | Think of two people you did the same for. See
yourself as possessing the qualities that inspire,
motivate, encourage and expand others.

3 | What qualities or character traits do you have that you would like to be able to express more of, such as compassion, wisdom, peace, joy, balance, security? State as many as you can think of below, and write each as if it is growing and expanding. For example, "My compassion is expanding every day."

4 | Select one person or situation in which to practice expressing one of those qualities this week.

VIII

Subpersonalities—
Uniting the
Separated Selves

The various roles and identities that you each have can be called your "subpersonalities." These roles exist within all of you. For instance, there may be a part of you that is impulsive and does things without thinking, and a part that is careful and cautious. There may be a part that does not like other people to be angry at you, or that wants to be needed by people. There may be a part of you that is afraid or creates fears of the future, or an obsessive part that remembers painful situations and calls them to your attention all the time. Each one of these parts, in the journey through this lifetime, is being brought to a higher level of knowing and understanding.

Learning not to identify with your subpersonalities as being the real you frees you and assists you in bringing them to the light. The journey into the higher self is the integration of all the selves, or subpersonalities, with the soul. The voice that tells you you cannot do something is not the voice of the higher self. It is simply a part of you that needs to be recognized and loved, to be shown your higher vision.

These selves that exist within you can be healed and integrated with your higher vision. Perhaps they were created during times of crisis, or they base their images of reality and their programs of instruction on pictures passed on to you from parents or friends. For instance, say you keep attracting what you feel are the wrong relationships into your life. There might be a self that is bringing you relationships based on an old image. Maybe your parents in some way rejected you, so a subpersonality formed an image of rejection as an element of being loved. This self may be very good at bringing you friends—so you must acknowledge that it is trying to do something positive for you, even though your friends at some point reject you. You must not make yourself wrong if you have a pattern you are creating over and over, for the clearing of that pattern is one of the ways you evolve. It is time now to bring this self into consciousness, talk to it, and give it a new image of what kind of love you want. You may have a self that believes in scarcity—that there are not enough men, or women, or enough love, money, etc. It would be good to talk to this part of you, showing it images of abundance.

Think for a moment, if you had six months to live, what would be the most important thing you would want to finish and leave behind? What would you change about your life right now? What limits do you have now that you would do away with? If you were to leave behind one gift to the planet, what would it be?

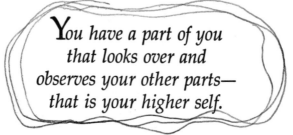

You have a part of you that looks over and observes your other parts— that is your higher self.

The greatest movement to the higher self comes both in acknowledging the higher self and in evolving all the other parts. Your subpersonalities are simply parts of you that are not yet aligned with your higher self. You can very easily change the images these parts are holding by first paying attention to the voices within you. When you hear a certain thought pattern, such as the voice that is doubtful, begin to see it as a part of you that is asking for help from your soul, a part that needs to be shown new images and belief systems. You can respond to any of the voices that you know are not your higher self by listening and speaking to them, telling them of your higher vision. They simply are not aware that you have changed the model by which you are creating reality.

What is this higher purpose, this higher vision? All of you came into incarnation not only to achieve certain levels of evolution, but to help with the planet, to be here as people contributing to the well-being of mankind. When things happen effortlessly and doors open, it is because you are not only on your own higher path, but you are weaving it into the higher vision of mankind. You are here to evolve certain qualities within yourself and to manifest your higher purpose. You can know what those qualities are by looking at what challenges continually present themselves to you. They may present themselves as separate situations, and yet there is a pattern to what you are learning in your life and the lessons you are attracting.

Everyone is born with a higher purpose and vision. You journey through this lifetime to find and fulfill that vision. The challenge to your higher self is to constantly enlarge your vision of who you are and to put that self in more and more expansive arenas. Some of you may specialize in one specific thing, focusing on it in more and more detail. For others your path may be to reach out into new areas for knowledge. It is the interweaving of all the parts within into the higher self that is one of the goals of soul in its evolutionary cycle.

The higher self is the part of you that is beyond the world of polarities. Every voice within you that is leaning in one direction will create its opposite. This means that if you have a part that is very conservative, that wants your life to stay the same, and does not like change, then there will be the opposite of that part—a part that likes to do things spontaneously, to be free and make changes. You may find these two parts constantly playing against each other.

You have many parts within you, one saying one thing, and always a part that says the opposite. Resolving these two sides allows the higher self to come through. One of the ways you can do this is to let the two parts carry on a dialogue. If you have a situation in your life in which you are going back and forth, saying with one part of you "This is the answer, handle it this way," and another part saying "No, it should be done *this* way," then you can look at it as if the two parts of you are in conflict. Imagine one of them in each hand, and create a dialogue between them. Let each of them express what good it is trying to do for you. Let each side talk to the other side, and explore a compromise that would work for both. Show them mentally what you are trying to accomplish with your life and ask them to help you with your important goals.

E*very single part of you has a gift for you and is there as your friend.*

There is no voice within you that does not have the intent to help you. It may be that it does not have an accurate picture of what you want, or it was set up many years ago and is still operating from an old program. The part of you that experiences fear, for instance, may be trying to protect you in the best way it knows. Your journey in this lifetime is to bring all those parts up into your higher vision and purpose.

Learn to love each of your selves, for as you love them you begin the process of uniting them with your higher self.

PLAYSHEET

1 | Take an area of your life in which you are experiencing a problem, or lack. Write it here.

2 | Now, decide which *part* of you is creating this lack. Close your eyes and imagine what this part looks like. Is it young or old? How is it dressed? What expressions does it have on its face?

3 | Thank this part of you for trying, in the best way it knows how, to do something good for you. Ask it what good thing it is trying to accomplish. For instance, the part of you that is holding you back may be trying to protect you and keep you safe. There is always something good this part thinks it is accomplishing. What good thing is it doing for you?

4 | Ask this part if it would be willing to do the same thing but in a different way, one that would contribute to your higher good and fit who you are now. You might ask that protective part to keep an eye on new ways to help you enter into a new challenge or adventure.

5 | Look again at this part of yourself. Does it look older, wiser, happier? Thank this part of you for being so willing to listen and help you with your higher goals.

IX

Love: Knowing the Wisdom of the Heart

Love is the food of the universe. It is the most important ingredient in life. Children go towards love, they thrive on love and grow on love, and would die without it. Love is an energy that circles the world; it exists everywhere and in everything. There is no one aspect of your life that does not involve love. Even the darkest moment has within it an element of love—the need for it, the lack of it, or the desire to create more. So much of the energy on this planet is directed toward having love, and yet so many thoughtforms exist about love in this and every culture that make love hard to have.

In speaking of love, I would like to speak of the common thoughts that exist about love. The thoughts people have about something are available to you telepathically, so when you are reaching for love, you are also pulling in the universal broadcast of it (along with all the mass beliefs that come with it).

Love is a feeling in the body, in the emotions, and ultimately in the spiritual realms. Love could be expressed as an omnipresent force, and can be seen as an element that holds together the particles in an atom. It is a force like gravity or magnetism, but it is not yet understood as a force. It can be expressed at the highest levels as a particle which is traveling so fast it is everywhere at once, and becomes all there is. All of you are striving for higher forms of love, but many of you get caught in the common thoughtforms that exist about it.

Imagine that there is a barrier to how much love you can absorb—such as the speed of light which has an upper limit. It has been said that nothing is faster than the speed of light, yet there is, though it is not yet known in your universe. It is the same with love, for on the earth plane there is a point of love that is the highest expression of it humanity as a whole has reached. Yet, even more love is possible. All of your great masters and teachers are working with a medium, a dimension of love, to bring more through to the earth plane. What would this love feel like? How would you know if you had it?

All of you have had an experience of that kind of love. You have words and terms about what love is, and yet you know love is more than words or thoughts. It is an experience, a knowing, a connection to another, to the earth, and ultimately to the higher self. In everything you connect with, there is a striving to reach a higher relationship with the self.

Often people offer you the opportunity to know your higher and better self through the platform of their love.

Yet, it seems as you strive for the higher realms of love, the personality frequently comes in with its doubts, fears, and expectations. To have more love you will need to break through your limitations. You can increase the love in your life by looking forward, letting go of your past patterns, and believing in your ability to love even more than you have ever loved in the past. Another way to have more love is to look backwards, remembering the times in which you were strong and loving and full of light. If you use the past to remember when it did not work, you will create your past limitations in your present relationships.

What does love bring up for most people? On a mass level, love brings up many pictures of form. In a relationship, it brings up commitment, marriage, ceremony, and ritual. In a family, it brings up taking care of others, being taken care of, dependence, and independence. It brings up attachment and detachment. On the personality level, love often brings up its opposite— fear. So many of you who have fallen in love or have had deep experiences of love find that afterwards you retract or contract, pulling away from the other person or withdrawing your love. The personality steps in and talks to you with its doubts and worries. You can deal with this by loving your personality and by reassuring it. Every time you walk through the doorway into more love, into a new dimension of love, you will always bring to the surface that part of you which has not felt loved. You may transfer it to the other person, blame it on her for pulling away, or create a situation in which you could not love him as much. But it is within you, it is you that creates the withdrawal. Rather than blame the other person when doubt or fear or disappointment comes up, look inward and ask, "Is there a part of me that is creating a reason to be afraid?" If you look inward and talk to that part, if you reassure it that there is nothing wrong with that fear, and show it the new and bright future you are going towards, you can walk even more in this place of love.

Imagine there are many telepathic messages that exist on your planet, and that whatever you think of, you tune in to all the other people who are thinking of the same thing. Now, if you are thinking of love, how loved you are, how much love there is in the universe, how light and joyful you feel, then you will tap in to all those other people who exist at that mind frequency. When doubts come up, they key you in to the thoughts and vibration of people who are living at that level of fear. Do not make those thoughts wrong, but do not dwell on them either. Don't spend time going over in your mind why something may not work, but instead focus upon how it *can* work, how much love you can offer everyone—your children, your parents, your friends, and those you love deeply and closely.

Love transcends the self.

All of you have had that experience of deep love, in which you were able to set aside your personality, your own wants and desires, to assist another. Love is a place that exists as an energy you can tap into whenever you have a loving thought of anyone. You literally pull up your own vibration. There are many high beings, such as I and those who work at this level, focusing love on the planet, so that your own feelings of love may be amplified. Any time you express unconditional love, from your deepest being, and any time you receive it, you assist many more people in achieving it also.

Love from the higher realms is absolute compassion and complete detachment. It is seeing the larger picture of people's lives and focusing upon not what you want from them, but how you can assist them in their unfoldment and growth in whatever direction is to their highest good. Love is focusing on how you may serve them, and in doing so, how you may serve your own growth and higher purpose. Love opens the doorway to your own growth and aliveness. You have witnessed how being in love has expanded your aliveness—being in love with anyone, be it a child, a parent, or a friend. The joy to me in coming through and assisting others is seeing the flower unfold, watching those I speak to grow and love themselves more. That energy comes back to me and is amplified many fold, so that I in turn am assisted even more in my broadcast of love.

Think for a moment of tomorrow. What is your day like tomorrow? Is there something you could do to give love to someone or to experience more love yourself tomorrow?

Acknowledging people and acknowledging yourself is another way to experience love. Taking a moment to appreciate everyone you see and to send them a feeling of love will change your life and raise your vibration rapidly. Being committed to the idea of love will bring it to you. You do not need to get into that personality level where you say, "Will this situation last, will it work?" Instead ask right now, "How can I deepen the love that I have in this relationship?" Love operates in the present, and by focusing upon it in the present, you send it into the future and release it to the past.

If you exist in a feeling of love—
if you can find it in everything you do,
transmit it through your touch,
through your words, eyes, and feelings—
you can cancel out with one act of love
thousands of acts of a lower nature.

You can help transform the planet. It does not take that many people focused on love to change the destiny of mankind, for love is one of the most powerful energies of the universe. It is thousands of times stronger than anger, resentment or fear.

For a moment, think of three people who could use your unconditional love, and send it to them. Imagine there are three people you would be willing to receive unconditional love from, and open to receive it.

Can you imagine how it would feel if your heart were open, if everywhere you went, you trusted, were relaxed, and knew that the universe was friendly? How would your life flow if you believed that your inner guidance was gentle and kind, and that people were sending you love wherever you went, and that you yourself broadcast a beam of love like a circle around you to everyone? How would your life change if whenever someone said something to you, no matter how it came out, you could recognize the love or need for love behind it? You would be constantly looking deeper to acknowledge and recognize the love within each being, as I do. By your recognition of love, you would bring it out and attract it to yourself.

As you go out to the world today, be aware of how you can express love through your eyes, through your smile, your heart, and even a gentle touch if it is appro-priate. You came to earth as a community and all of you can send out a high loving feeling, a thoughtform of love, and offer it to each other. For the rest of today, be in your heart. Experience the love that is you, and as you do, be open to receive the acknowledgement of the beautiful light and love within you from others.

PLAYSHEET

1 | List at least three times in the past when you felt a surge of loving feelings as you thought of or talked to someone, or gave him or her love:

2 | Think of three people who could use your love. Recall those loving feelings you had in step 1 above. Send that love out to these three people.

3 | Write here three times someone gave you love that was unexpected.

4 | Think of some way you could surprise and delight someone tomorrow with an expression of your love.

X

*O*pening *to* *R*eceive

Imagine, if you will, that you are a king, and your treasury is full. In fact, you have so much you do not know where to begin distributing the wealth. All of the people in your kingdom are walking around saying how poor they are, but when you offer them your money they act as if they do not see you, or they wonder what is wrong with what you are offering.

I look out and see the storehouses all over—untapped, unused and even unrecognized. You have heard the expression "Heaven on Earth." There is nothing that stops you from having it, except your ability to ask for and receive it. What are these storehouses? What things lie within them that we would love to pass out?

One is love. We do not measure growth as you do (career advancements, more money, etc.). We look to spiritual evolution, which includes joy, self-love, the ability to receive, reframing the negative into the positive, the refinement of the ego, a willingness to embrace the new, and the ability to work together for common purpose.

There is so much love available,
it is as abundant as the air you breathe.

Do you ask for love? The more you give and receive love the greater your spiritual growth. Every moment you spend focused on something that is not working, thinking of someone who does not love you, makes you like the men who turn away from the King's money. You always have the opportunity to think of times you were loved, imagine a future of abundance, and thus partake of spiritual wealth.

What do you think of? Every in-breath takes you up to the world of essence where form is created, and on the out-breath you send to the world your wishes. Every time you recognize the love you have, you increase it. One of the laws of receiving is that recognizing when you have gotten something increases it in your life, and every time you do not acknowledge something you make it so much harder to have more sent to you.

The more you focus on what is wrong, the more wrong you will create in your life; the more it will spread to other areas that WERE working. The more you concentrate on what is right in your life, what is working, the more other areas of your life will work. It is the same in receiving. The more you acknowledge how much you are receiving, the more you will have.

We have here two kinds of requests: those made by your personality, and those made by your soul.

What are the requests of your soul?

A request for spiritual evolution is a soul request, as is a request for higher purpose: clarity, love, and focus. A desire to find your higher path or for more light in your life is also a soul request.

Personality requests can be the clothing of a soul request. They are usually more specific, the request for a new car or a material object, for instance. If you are willing to look at the deeper motivation behind what you want, and what you expect to get from having it, then you will open up many more ways and forms in which it can come to you.

A personality request is very specific so it often takes longer for the universe to find ways to get it to you. If, however, instead of asking for money, you ask for what the money would bring you, such as more security, the ability to travel, to take time off from your job, or pay your bills every month with ease, all of those can be brought to you more easily than the money.

Learning to receive is learning to ask for the essence of what you want, rather than the form.

Often the universe brings what you specifically ask for and you find it isn't what you want. This wastes much time. Before you say that you want something, ask, "Is there any broader or more accurate way I can state that request?"

When you say, "I want this man or woman to love me" or "I want this person to bring me joy," then you have made it very difficult for the universe to give you what you want, especially if they do not love you or bring you joy. If instead you say, "I am open to receiving a man or woman who will love me," then it is much easier to have it, for you are not attached to the form, (a specific person) but rather to the essence (love and joy).

If you want something to appear in a specific way, it may take longer than if you let the universe create magic and miracles and bring you the soul request, rather than the personality desire. Often, this requires the ability to let go and detach.

You may have experienced picturing something and having it come to you. Yet many of you don't know how to let go of the old and open to the new. Be willing to be open to new forms if you want to receive.

If your life is cluttered with many relationships, for instance, or if you are filling your time with an unsatisfying relationship, then there is no room left in your life for a fulfilling one. If you are asking for more money but you are spending all your time giving away your services, or pursuing activities that do not bring you money, it will be much more difficult to attract it.

B*e willing to do what your soul directs
you to do if you want to create
what you are asking for.*

Health

Often when you ask for something, you will find yourself going through unexpected changes to prepare you for having it. It may be that your attitude needs changing, or it may be that the viewpoint you are holding actually creates an energy block to your attracting that gift. The universe will immediately send you many experiences to open up and change your attitude, so that you can have what you requested.

Sometimes you must let go of certain things to have what you have asked for. It may be that you need to release a thought, friend, useless activity, or a high level of worry. It is not that the universe is punishing you, or trying to make it hard for you to get what you want, but that you have a gentle and loving inner teacher that wants to give things to you only when you are ready, and when it will be for your highest good.

A lot of money may be withheld, for instance, if you are not ready to handle it. Your higher self may bring you many lessons to change and shift your attitudes before money comes, so that it will truly benefit your growth. If you are asking for things egotistically, the universe will always prepare you so that you will not be harmed by having it. Many requests for fame and great amounts of money are not actually to the benefit of the soul and may therefore be slowed down.

You ask for so little, and that is what saddens us as we look over the minds of men. We see the limited focus of your thoughts, looking so close at hand rather than reaching for the heights.

There are ways to have more in your life.

One is to use your imagination, for it is a great gift you have been given. Every time you imagine having something, challenge yourself—imagine having even more! If you want a house, a friend, or lover, any relationship, a car, a life of leisure—fantasize about it, and enlarge the vision.

Fantasy can lead to higher purpose. For many of the things you fantasize about the most (even those you feel furthest from having) are pictures of your higher purpose and the life you will lead as you reach it.

What can you ask for? You can ask for spiritual evolution and more light, for that is a general request that will be utilized by your soul to bring many unexpected gifts. (You will want to acknowledge these gifts when they come.)

> *Trust yourself and believe*
> *you can create what you want.*

Having faith in yourself, and letting go of those memories of times when things did not work will help you open to more abundance. If you must think of the past, think of those times you were powerful and creative. Go into your heart and ask whether you feel you deserve all the joy and love that is awaiting you on your path of higher purpose.

You can begin to imagine joy, peace and harmony as your birthright. Focus, clarity, and love are available for the asking. Request a vision of your higher purpose, and be willing to recognize the gifts every day as they come, even the small things. The more you acknowledge what is being sent to you, the more you can bring into your life.

Ask! We cannot give you anything unless you ask. The universe waits for you to ask. When you see it coming, be willing to take and receive it. When the opportunity comes, grab it! Thank and acknowledge the universe for it, and you can create Heaven on Earth.

PLAYSHEET

1 | List at least 4 things in your life you are doing well, things that are working and you are feeling good about:

2 | What good things have you received from the universe in the last week or month? List at least 10 things:

3 | Think of at least 5 things you asked for in the past
and received:

4 | What would you like to receive from the universe
now? State your requests with precision. Use your
imagination and *ask* for all you can think of. Example: I would like to receive an income of $2,000 *or
more* a month starting within 6 months, or sooner,
and earn it in a way that facilitates my higher purpose.

XI

Appreciation, Gratitude, and the Law of Increase

If you want to come out of a bad space, if you are drained or depleted, if you have been around someone who upset you, then you can quickly change your energy by looking at the good things you have and saying thanks—thank you *self*, thank you *Universe*. It is an effective way of cleaning your aura and raising your vibration. If you were to wake up each morning and spend two minutes giving thanks, you would find yourself having a much higher day.

What is the purpose of gratitude? It is not just something you have to do because your parents told you to say thank you and be polite. You have a holiday called Thanksgiving; you have heard of people who give thanks after coming through an ordeal. There is a higher reason for gratitude and thanks. They literally send out a call to the Universe to give you more.

Whatever you appreciate and
give thanks for
will increase in your life.

Have you ever noticed how much you like to be with people who thank you, appreciate and acknowledge you? When you give them advice, they say "Thank you, that helps so much." When you offer them something, they hold it and love it. Have you noticed how you want to give them more? It is the same, on an energy level, with the Universe. Whenever you stop to thank the Universe for the abundance you have, the Universe will give you more. Whenever you give thanks, you increase the light in your aura at that very moment. You change it through your heart, for the feeling of gratitude comes from the heart. As you give thanks, you open your heart. Your heart is the doorway to your soul; it is the link between the world of form and the world of essence. Gratitude and thanks are a path straight to the heart, to your essence and your soul.

You can clean your aura and raise your vibration by giving thanks. The resonance of gratitude in your body vibrates with your heart center. It allows you to open to receive more. It opens your heart to your consciousness, healing the physical body with its radiance of love. It sets up a higher, finer vibration, and it is your vibration that magnetizes you to the things you want. When you give thanks, the Universe sets up a matching note or sound that brings you even more of the same.

There are various methods of expressing thanks—mental, verbal, and written. And, there is the emotional, heartfelt sense of gratitude, which is the most important. No matter how you give thanks, if it is done idly, without paying attention and feeling it in your heart, then it is not as effective as when you are fully aware and coming from true gratitude. When you *think* a "Thank you," it does have an effect on your body, and it is even more powerful to say it aloud. Have you been around people who constantly thank you? I am not speaking of those who do it from habit or because they are always apologizing or wanting your favor. I am referring to people who truly acknowledge and appreciate you when you are with them. These people are increasing what they will receive from other people and from the world.

The process of writing ideas down and speaking them puts them out into the world of form more quickly than just thinking them. If you want something, write it down or say it out loud, because the processes of speech and writing are one step closer to having something than the process of thinking. The hands and the throat are two centers of manifestation. The ideas in your mind, when expressed to others, become part of the world of form, and when written on paper are even closer to being created. It is all right to express thanks in your mind. That will evolve you also, but it is even more powerful to say it out loud to the Universe and others. The written thank you is even more powerful than the spoken.

To *create something new, or to keep receiving more of something you have already gotten, get some paper and pens and write a thank you to the Universe.*

At night, make a list of everything you received during the day. It may be something you bought, a smile from a stranger, a good feeling or extra energy, a car that got you where you wanted to go or money you received. You will be amazed at all the gifts that are sent your way every day. In acknowledging what you received, you will create a connection with the universe that will allow you to have even more.

You may want to write or call someone who has helped you and express your appreciation. The more you express outwardly your gratitude and thankfulness for what you have, the more you change your molecular vibration away from the dense energy into finer levels. You may notice that highly evolved souls and great teachers spend much of their time appreciating and thanking the Universe. In their meditation they feel true humility and gratitude for every thing they are given.

What is the effect of gratitude on the various bodies? The physical body literally undergoes a change when you are appreciative. When you acknowledge your good health, for instance, you send a message to the cells in your body. They respond to it, for each of your cells has within it the hologram of the whole of you. Each cell has an awareness of its own. (Not that they think in the ways you know.) You are composed of many different cells which function at a level of awareness that is not the same as the overall awareness you call "I." They like to be appreciated also. If you want to heal a problem in your body, instead of remembering those times when you weren't healthy, or worrying about future pains or problems, thank your body for all the wonderful things it is doing well. If you send it gratitude frequently you will find it doing even more for you. The cells definitely do understand the feeling of gratitude and will try to work for you even harder.

Find appreciation for how well your body moves, acts and gets you around. Appreciate how it converts your food into energy and how well it serves you. On the other hand, if you look at your body and make it wrong, saying "I don't like my thighs, stomach, etc.," if you complain about it, you will find that it does not respond as well. Think of your body as containing millions of little entities—cells—that have feelings. The minute you make up your mind you appreciate them, you change your physical vibration. The cells immediately go to work to increase your energy. When you have a negative thought, one of ingratitude, then your energy drops.

Gratitude is healing to the emotions.

It links the emotional body to the heart and thus to the soul, which is reached through the heart. The emotional body is a restless, constantly vibrating flow of energy around you. When you say thanks, and appreciate your life, acknowledging people, events, and the higher forces, the pattern of energy that represents your emotional body begins to rearrange itself into a higher and finer vibration. Your emotions are the most magnetic part of you when it comes to attracting events, people and objects. The calmer and more detached you are, the easier it is to have what you want. Your will and intent will need to be directed towards having it. The more peaceful and serene you are, the more easily you can focus on your higher being and the more you can have.

When you experience emotionally a sense of deep gratitude, it is calming and effective in raising the vibration of your emotional body. The heart is most affected and most easily reached by gratitude. If you want to link with another in your heart, appreciate him or her. By sending out your telepathic appreciation, you will automatically stop power struggles. When you see friends this week, notice and acknowledge something good about them. Be sure it is heartfelt, and not something you have to make up. If you can find something to say to them that is gratitude for who they are, you will immediately move the level of contact up into the heart.

Giving thanks and appreciation opens many doors into the higher levels of the Universe.

Appreciation is a doorway into the heart, it opens your heart and allows you to experience more love in your life. In the next week, appreciate each person you see when you remember to do so. If it is your friend or a loved one, a stranger or co-worker, see if you can send him or her gratitude and thanks. Appreciate something about that person from your heart. Gratitude takes you out of your head and judgment. Many of you are wrapped up in your thoughts, and when you give thanks, it takes you out of that mental place of right and wrong, good and bad, and puts you into your heart. When you get out of your mind level, even for a short time, it is possible for the Universe to work more directly with you. Often the level of mental activity that is going on in all of you creates so much confusion it is harder for you to get what you want.

When appreciation is felt in the mental body (the part of you that thinks all the time), it literally silences the worry part, the doubting or skeptical side. It brings together all your selves under a new banner, and can be a doorway into a new level of energy. Whenever you find yourself upset or concerned, experiencing something that does not feel healing, stop and give thanks for the good things you have.

A feeling of gratitude allows you access to your abstract mind, which is the part of you that links the right and left brain, male and female sides. The abstract mind does not work only with the left-brain side, which deals with numbers, figures, and logic, nor does it work specifically with the right-brain side, which deals with creativity, intuition and feelings. It synthesizes these two parts. The union comes when you are able to conceptualize with frameworks of beliefs and realities that are outside your normal way of thinking. It feels like a light coming through, a new solution to an old problem, an inspiration or revelation.

The abstract mind is able to see the larger picture of your life, and you spend so little time there. This part of you has many new ways of thinking; it exists beyond the normal framework you live in. The abstract mind does not think in terms you are used to. It is the genius level that exists within all of you. It uses the highest form of thinking you have and it can greatly assist you in evolving if you are willing to use it more often.

You can choose to think in
a higher way more often.

Giving thanks will lead you directly to your heart and your abstract mind. By giving thanks, you bring light into your crown center at the top of your head, through the doorway of your heart. Because of the increased light, and new heart opening, many ideas and gifts can be sent to you. They may unfold in a week, or month, but you have created a doorway for many good things to come to you. Imagine that gratefulness allows you to reach into and change your vibration, to go to the higher levels of wisdom that are available in the Universe. The Universe hears your call; thank you's are definitely heard and appreciated, and you will be sent that energy back.

All of you have desires, and desires make up what I call your "desire body." There are things that you want to have in your life. If I asked you what you desire, what is most important to have right now, you could tell me if you stopped and thought about it. When you give thanks, you affect your desire body. The desire body is quite restless, like the emotional body. It is always focusing on what it does not have and what it wants to create. It has a purpose, for it brings you new forms, motivation and creative energy. Yet, it can bring you a sense of runaway energy—reminding you of all the things you have yet to do and create.

Your desires can seem overwhelming, if you have too many unfulfilled ones. Giving thanks directly affects desires by allowing them to calm down and to see how much they have created. Think of it as if you have a separate part of you composed of those things you have been wanting. When you give thanks, it empowers this part. For this self does not usually focus on what you have generated, but wants to tell you what you could do, how much harder you could work, and on and on.

It always has lists of things for you to do, and it needs to be reassured, talked to, and calmed down. Feeling appreciation for what you have done will accomplish this, and will strengthen this part in its ability to create more.

Another body is that of the will. All of you have different pictures of will. Some of you call it "Will Power."

> *Will is the ability to direct your energy where you want it to go.*

Many of you want to go higher, into the finer levels of energy where there is more peace, joy, contentment, and detachment. The will is energy that flows through you constantly. It is like a stream or river of energy that moves through you all the time. When you give thanks, you strengthen your will. Not will power, but will that is linked with the heart, will that is directed to doing what you love. The more you appreciate yourself, acknowledge everything in your life, the more you link your heart with your will. This allows you to create those things your heart has been wanting.

APPRECIATION, GRATITUDE, AND THE LAW OF INCREASE
PLAYSHEET

1 | What things do you appreciate having in your life right now?

2 | What people do you appreciate?

3 | What good things about yourself—your body,
mind, etc.—do you appreciate?

Ideas:
Call someone on the phone or write and express your
appreciation of him or her.

You can begin to experience various levels of inner peace, down to the deepest feelings of it. Start by finding a sense of peace within you. Give yourself one opportunity in the next week to feel inner peace. You may want to create a place of beauty, a sense of timelessness, provide music, so that you can truly experience what peace means to you. From that space, from that knowing, you can begin to change everything you see in the outer world.

What is the value of inner peace? Certainly it feels better to the emotional body. But it is more than that—it is the ability to affect the outer world from your highest level, to create and manifest from a focused place of purpose and an inner sense of who you are. When you are tranquil and calm, when you slow down and feel relaxed, you are able to create and think at your higher levels. What you bring to earth and create from this space is your higher good.

You can create things when you feel tense, anxious or fearful, but those things may not be for your highest good; in fact, they will probably not be. If, before you plan your life or think of new ideas you find a sense of inner peace and operate from it, you will find your plans reflecting more of your soul's purpose than your personality desires. If before you act or speak you bring in this sense of peace, you will find your world changing rapidly into a very different place.

*Inner peace is a connection
to your deeper self,
and it will assist you
in letting go of fear.*

Fear is a lower energy, a vibration of less light, and can be changed by love. One of the goals of having inner peace is healing fear. It may be a fear that someone will hurt or reject you, abandon or run away from you. It may be a fear that you cannot make it in the world, a fear of putting yourself out there and failing. Inner peace is a connection to the heart and a willingness to let go of fear. It is achieved by letting go of having anything to defend, and being willing to be vulnerable. It is not putting on an act for other people; it is being willing to shine through as who you are, and knowing you are all right.

Having inner peace means committing to letting go of self-criticism and self-doubt. Everything other people say to you about yourself is a reflection of a voice within you. What other people say to you also reflects how they speak to themselves. If you find people critical, first ask, is there a part of you that is criticizing yourself? As you let go of that self-criticism, you will experience less criticism from others. Remember also that what people say to you is a reflection of who they are and how they see the world. They may criticize you because they are critical of themselves. See their actions and words as a statement of their beliefs and learn to remain calm and centered.

Inner peace heals. You do not need to focus on your fears to let go of them. By achieving a feeling of inner peace, holding any situation in your life up to the light, you will find your mind opening to new ideas, solutions and answers that come from your soul. Inner peace is the connection to your spiritual self. You achieve it through physical relaxation in the body, emotional calm, and mental focus on higher ideals and qualities. If you wish to go upward, to experience and live in the higher levels of energy, inner peace is the doorway.

Once you decide to create inner peace, you may find many things happening that challenge your resolve to remain peaceful. You may say, "I can remain peaceful *except* if *that* happens." The universe is sending you those exceptions as an opportunity to create a new response of peace instead of being upset.

How do you manifest inner peace and hold it steadily? You begin by acknowledging those moments when you have inner peace, attuning your awareness to the feeling, and by having the will and intent to create it. You can use your imagination to think of what it would feel like. You can think about or contemplate inner peace, for wherever you place your thoughts you begin to create experience.

*You can decide
to stop being affected by
the outer world and, instead,
to affect the world around
with your peace.*

No matter what happens each day, if unexpected bills arrive in the mail or someone changes his mind, no matter what in the past has destroyed your emotional calm, mental peace, or physical well-being, decide that you will now radiate peace, healing, and love. The world you see around you is but an illusion created by the energy you are sending out. Anything is possible. The limits you see, the part of you that says "this can't be done" are only thoughts. They absolutely can be changed. From a position of inner peace you can create the reflection of your soul's light in the outer world.

Manifesting inner peace means acting rather than reacting. It is a stance, an attitude; it is an energy you send flowing outward into the world. It means you can connect with the universe at your higher soul levels. Imagine there are many streams of energy around you, and you can choose to operate in any one you wish. One is called struggle, a great deal of work to get what you want, and another is called joy. When you're anxious, tense and worried, you are in the first stream. If for even a moment you find inner peace, you automatically join the second, higher flow of energy.

There are many people alive right now who are creating and experiencing energy flows of creativity, peace, and light. Whenever you achieve inner peace, you link with all those beings that are living in and creating this higher energy flow. Ideas may begin to come to you. You can pull in anything you need from this position of peace.

To have inner peace, you will need to be willing to open your heart. When something happens that would normally make you feel defensive or closed, when you would normally pull away choosing to feel hurt, you have another choice. If instead you are willing to open your heart just one more notch, experience a little more compassion and understanding for other people, you will find yourself able to send them love and create a feeling of peace for yourself.

*You can choose to see
the world any way
you want.*

You may say "Yes, but this is the way my life is, these are the facts. If only this situation changed, or I had more money, or this person would stop irritating me, I could discover inner peace." What you experience as real is simply a reflection of your belief systems and your mind. If you choose to experience inner peace anyway, you can change everything you now experience as real—bringing in new ideas and beliefs that might work in higher and better ways.

Forgiveness is necessary for inner peace. If there are people from your past you hold a grudge against, or feel negatively towards, you can in a few minutes forgive them and let go. If someone hasn't returned your call or letter, owes you something, or hurt you badly, you will clear your own energy if you forgive, let go and detach. Inner peace means releasing attachments to anything—to having a person act the way you want or to having the world work the way you expect. When you let go of those attachments, you will find your life working even better than you could have expected or planned. It does not mean giving up control of your life; it means coming from your own center of peace at all times.

Right now, make the decision that you can bring inner peace into your life. Make the decision that you're going to open your heart even more, be more compassionate, more understanding, more loving, and more forgiving of everyone you know. Form a picture in your mind of yourself going through the next week, and see yourself coming from a totally new level of peace. See the smile on your face and the joy in your heart.

Take one thing in your life that you would like to feel peace about, something that possibly you have been reacting to, and make a mental image of releasing, forgiving and letting go, finding inner peace with this issue. Only you can create inner peace. From that space, you will see the world you experience reflecting it. Other people, events, and situations do not need to trigger a reaction in you. If, instead, you maintain this center of peace, you will change those events that used to disturb and upset you. If they do not change, it will no longer intrude on your sense of well-being. You can find your center, your soul's light and your inner being reflected and carried out in the world you experience.

FEELING INNER PEACE
PLAYSHEET

Relax your body. Take three deep breaths and let all tension go.

1 | Remember three times you felt inner peace. Really experience that peaceful feeling. Write about them here.

2 | What things take away your peaceful feeling? Finish this sentence: I can be peaceful except . . . (For example, "except when my boss is in a bad mood.")

3 | Say to yourself, "The part of me that doesn't feel peaceful is only a small part and I now identify and connect with my strong inner self. This strong side is now putting more light into that small fearful part."

4 | Now take every statement above and turn it into a positive affirmation—"My strong inner self feels peace even when my boss is in a bad mood." As you do so, let yourself feel the strength of your wise, confident self, and then release, forgive and let go of each situation that is a distraction to your inner peace.

XIII

Achieving Balance, Stability, and Security

You can create stability by calming down and taking a few moments to think before you act. Continuous action without pause is appropriate for some of the tasks you have to do and inappropriate if done all the time.

As you move through the day many of you engage in continuous motion, going from one thing to the next as each comes across your mind or catches your eye. If you wish to feel stable and balanced, stop often throughout the day and focus on what you are doing. Change your perspective. Sit quietly and experience yourself and your thoughts from a calmer level of awareness. This involves bringing your emotions into a state of peace and quiet. When you change your position and sit down, putting your hands at your sides, you change your breathing. When there is no motion in your body other than your thoughts, you can think in a different way.

You may begin to experience a greater connection to your higher self at this time. As you pause for a moment in your daily activities, resting your body, quieting your mind and calming your emotions, you will discover many new ways to look at what is happening in your life. When you are continuously in motion you think differently from when you sit down and get quiet. Quieting your physical body enables your spirit to come into your thoughts, particularly as you become peaceful and serene.

Balance and stability are achieved by checking with your higher self before taking action, especially on important issues. That means giving yourself the opportunity to view things from many different angles before acting. It means allowing yourself to take whatever time is necessary to do a good job. Many things that take you off balance can be avoided by giving yourself enough time to think before you act. There is a saying, "Look before you leap." You do not need to stop before every action you take, but you can make your life much easier and more joyful if you stop and think about something important before you take action. It may be the purchasing of a new car or the signing of a contract. All changes can bring balance and peace when viewed with careful thought. If you are in continuous motion, you can end up making decisions and taking actions that lead to crisis and problems.

If you have a decision to make about something you consider important, don't rush into it. As you allow yourself time to think about it, you live out many probable futures in your mind, and you begin to see the consequences of certain actions. One of the gifts of your world is that it is a place of action and reaction. Whenever you take an action you set ripples into motion, like the ripples on a pond when you throw in a stone. Every action affects probable futures and makes changes in your life path. The more you can anticipate what things will be affected by your action and take action from that perspective of greater wisdom, the more you will set up joy and balance in your future.

Your attitude determines how you experience the world.

It is the way you react to certain things. An attitude that creates joy is one in which you interpret what happens to you through the filter of joy. Your attitude and outlook act like a filter. When you have a positive, optimistic outlook, it filters out the negative and denser experiences.

Your attitude is the words you use when you talk to yourself. Perhaps you have just succeeded in achieving a goal you have wanted to accomplish. A joyful attitude says, "Congratulations, job well done." If your joyful self speaks words of praise it helps you bring more of the same to yourself. Attitudes are magnetic and every moment you spend in joy magnetizes another moment of joy. Joyful, light emotions are always more powerful in their ability to create than negative emotions.

Stability comes from an attitude of balance. When things happen to you, your response to them creates your inner balance. If a friend is having problems and you respond by feeling angry or sad, you have moved away from your own center and allowed your friend's energy to affect you.

As you begin to create more balance and stability in your life, you will be able to observe when you are affected by other people's problems. It is most noticeable when those problems have no impact on your life, do not affect you directly, and yet you are still depressed or upset. Observe those situations in which your balance is disturbed by another's lack of balance. The next step is to tell yourself that you can keep your balance, that you are not dependent upon others responding in a balanced way for you to remain centered and balanced.

Many of you have allowed yourselves to respond in an unstable or insecure way when someone around you is acting that way. When someone is speaking to you about something you did wrong, or accusing you of something, instead of feeling angry you can choose to keep your sense of balance even though the other person is not able to do so. As his energy comes into you and you begin to feel it unbalancing you, see that you are resonating with that unbalanced part in him. To stop responding in this way, send him love. As you do so you reassert your own balance and connect with your higher self.

Balance is finding the midway point between opposites. You are always involved in maintaining balance, both literally in the mechanism of the inner ear and symbolically through the juggling of all the things in your life. Whatever you picture balance to be, it will be.

You create balance by visualizing balance, and by being clear that those pictures of balance are what you want.

Some of you define balance as boring, for you thrive on things being slightly out of balance, creating drama and intense emotions. You have seen people whose lives are in constant upset, who go from one crisis to another. What they picture as balance is moving back and forth between extremes.

To some the thought of balance and stability means a void of emotions, something that can seem frightening. As you reach higher planes of reality, your emotions become so calm they are like the still lake that reflects back every cloud and tree. Many people, however, fear having no feelings, and they will create anything to get attention rather than have no attention paid them at all. Often people create upset and problems all around them because they are afraid that if everything were calm no one would pay attention to them. They would rather have negative attention than no attention at all.

Some of you depend on intense emotions to feel alive. Yet intense, dramatic emotions always take you away from your center. Some of you, when you are feeling very peaceful, having little emotion, think you are sad or depressed. Whenever you get silent within, do you begin to think that something is wrong? Are you addicted to strong, intense emotions? Do you feel good when things are peaceful and calm or do you begin to worry about what will go wrong next? It takes patience to get used to being calm. Although you might think it would be easy, it is harder for most people to adapt to a peaceful environment than to a disruptive one. If the environment is too peaceful, many will begin to create turbulence because it is what they are used to.

People need different things to maintain their balance. Some people need a steady job, some require large blocks of time off, and others need much activity and constant variety. Go within for a moment and picture a time in your life when you felt stable and balanced. If you cannot think of a time, think of a symbol to represent the balance you would like in your life. Now picture yourself feeling balanced in the future. Having a symbol to represent something is a very powerful way to draw it to you. Symbols work on a deeper level of consciousness than words and bypass belief systems.

Balance is about moderation and not extremes. Maintaining balance in your life means doing the right amount of each thing. Some of you think that things would be better if you only had more time off. Yet, when people retire they find that there is such a thing as too much time off. There is a balance between work and play, sleep and wakefulness, time together and time apart that will create the most peace and joy for you. It is not eliminating opposites that brings balance. It is doing things in moderation, stopping when the energy is gone and riding the waves as they come in. It means pacing yourself in a steady, even way.

Some of you keep going long after the energy to do something has left. Do those things that bring aliveness to you. There is a proper mix of focus and daydreaming, intellect and intuition, sitting and movement which brings joy. Most of you need variety and all of you need to keep growing. Balance is finding the proper mix of activities that support your aliveness and allow you to most joyfully accomplish your purpose.

Some people feel balanced when they feel peaceful, others feel balanced when they create excitement, when things are moving rapidly in their lives and they are busy juggling many things. Some picture balance as things going well and under control. You are constantly creating the degree of balance you will have in the future by the pictures you have of yourself in the future.

*True security exists
when all needs can be met
by the self.*

Most of you think that to have security you must find something or somebody in the outer world who will give you something that will make you feel secure. No one can give you anything before you give it to yourself. If you cannot give it to yourself then no one can give it to you either. This means that anything you are seeking right now to feel secure—such as money, a boyfriend or girlfriend, marriage, a home—none of those will fulfill that need until you have given yourself inner security.

Some of the things people think they need to feel secure are acknowledgement and recognition, praise, love, fame and fortune. Often love is demanded from others in a very specific way—so many phone calls a week, so many hugs, so many times the other person says "I love you." Security needs can also include the need to feel the world is safe, to feel that you are special, to feel a part of something. Many of you look to others to give this to you, and you find constant disappointment. You can satisfy your security needs yourself—you can love yourself, believe that the world is safe, acknowledge and recognize your accomplishments. Ultimately, only the self can fulfill these needs.

Many of you, in your search for a higher purpose, select other people and their lives as your purpose. You want to get wrapped up in their lives, draw them close to you, have them listen to your every word, cater to your slightest whim, and be swept off your feet, as they say. The desire to become entwined in another person's life, being more involved in their future than yours, can cover up the need to fulfill your own higher purpose. When you seek to feel secure by making another person your project before you have made your own growth a priority, you will find constant disappointment in the outcome. At the very least you will find that the need for self-growth cannot be met by making another's growth your life's work.

Security comes from having something in your life that is bigger than yourself, something you are reaching for, something that attracts and pulls and calls to you. It makes the petty hurts and insignificant events small by comparison. And yet, many of you seek that bigger thing in each other, rather than in your own growth.

> To *feel secure you need to feel*
> *you are growing, expanding, and*
> *enlarging the scope of your world.*

You might think you will feel more secure by keeping things unchanged, maintaining the status quo. Yet, security only comes from taking a risk, opening up, and discovering more of who you are. Some people have discovered when they try to keep their world safe by not taking risks they end up even more scared and insecure. Fear is always lessened when you face it. You may have noticed when you did something new you felt braver and stronger in other areas also.

Balance is handling the amount of things you have to deal with every day in a way that is peaceful and healthy to you, and in a way that contributes to your growth and higher good. It keeps the things you are doing stimulating, helping you to wake up in the morning feeling that life is worthwhile. Decide that you will become a radiating source of stability and balance for those around you. Give yourself the things you require for joy and be willing to accept a peaceful universe when it comes.

PLAYSHEET

1 | Think of an important issue in your life right now.
It may be a large purchase, changing jobs, ending a
relationship. Record it here.

2 | Sit quietly and relax your body. Let your deep inner
feelings surface. Spend at least five minutes thinking about this issue. Ask for guidance from your
higher self and the higher forces of the universe.
Record any new thoughts that come up here.

3 | Stay in this quiet, relaxed state. Think about what you could do right now to bring more balance and stability into your life. Record your ideas here.

4 | Create a symbol for balance and stability in your mind or draw it below. Imagine that it is growing and expanding and becoming more powerful.

XIV

Clarity:
Living in More Light

Achieving clarity involves seeing the larger picture, a longer time frame, a bigger perspective. The larger your view, the clearer you can be. The ability of a great master to know the purpose of a soul in this lifetime brings clarity of vision and advice. How can you develop this kind of clarity in your own life?

Most of you are in a time frame that involves thinking of weeks and days, rather than years, rather than looking from the perspective of your entire life span, of your time here on earth. If you are willing to look at yourself as a whole, you can begin to find different levels of clarity around the present moment. It does not mean you need to know the form or where you are going. It means that the larger the picture you hold of who you are, the clearer you can be. If you were to go into the future and look back at today, you could gain a new perspective of who you are, for clarity is brought about by the changing of perspective. Most of you have certain ways you think, certain habits and patterns. Every time you break free and find a new way of thinking, you increase clarity.

Clarity is not something that you reach and have from then on. It is an ongoing refinement of your picture. Imagine a boat trying to find a place to land near the shore. There is heavy fog, and the men in the boat cannot see anything, so they do not leave the boat nor do they take any action. As the fog lifts and they continue to look, they begin to see the fuzzy outline of the horizon and the shore. But still, they do not know what is there, so they do not take any action. Pretty soon, as the fog begins to dissolve, the picture becomes clear. They now know what lies ahead, and so they prepare for action. It is the same process with clarity. At first, ideas seem vague and foggy, for that is the way essence becomes form. As the perceptual process begins, a new idea or a new way of looking at things emerges, vague in form. Often it is only a sense that something you have now is not right. It may start as an uncomfortable feeling, for the process of gaining clarity is also the process of letting go of confusion. It may be a longing, a desire, a want or a need. It will become part of your emotional awareness after it passes through your perceptions.

Things do not usually suddenly become clear, as there is an ongoing process to clarity. When you first feel that vague dissatisfaction, that sense that something needs to be changed, ask yourself, "How can I fine-tune this picture?" The more precise you can be about your experience, the more quickly you will gain clarity. Take any area of vague discomfort, of fogginess, and focus upon it to the exclusion of all other thoughts.

Pin down precisely what the uncomfortable feeling is. If you were to focus upon that vagueness, putting words to it, trying out different thoughts about it, you would finally find a viewpoint that clicked. Once you find that viewpoint, you have clarity. Clarity comes from seeking and finding the information you need, from having the patience to seek out the light of wisdom that will assist in the higher choice.

Clarity often involves a way of looking at things that puts them into a usable format, that fits them with and adjusts them to who you are, so you may proceed with action. Action is always preceded by a decision, and a decision is arrived at through clarity, if you are operating from your highest level.

What is the value of clarity? What will it do for you to be clear? It will save you much time; in fact, it can save years of being on a slower path of evolution. Being clear means taking the time to think out issues in your life. It is more important to think them out than to act them out. Many of you want to take action, to see results. Finding right action is quite easy if you are willing to spend the time to think, to pull in your higher, finer self, to concentrate, and to create the space to do it.

> Clarity comes from a
> state of mental concentration,
> of focusing the thoughts,
> and paying attention.

Clarity is reached by training the mind to be precise and accurate in its definition of experience. Clarity means that you are focused and living at a level of energy that others cannot interfere with. The clearer your energy is, the less affected you will be by other people, the less touched you will be by other people's expectations or desires, and the clearer will be your path in life. You need clarity not just to carry out your life's purpose, but in every area of your life.

Be *clear* on your intent. What do you intend to do with your life? To grow? To be happy? To be joyful? To serve, to heal? The higher the level of clarity you can begin with, the more that energy will flow down into every area of your life. Your life purpose is the most important thing you can get clear on. Clarity of purpose will direct clear energy into every other area of your life. You may say "What is life purpose, in essence?" It is that deepest desire within you, that which gives you the most joy, that which you think of, fantasize about all the time. It is that deep soul-level urge, that motivation; it is the dream that you hold within you.

The next level of clarity after the level of life purpose is clarity of intent. How do you intend to carry out your life purpose? Even more importantly, do you intend to do it? Clarity of intent is the picture, the vision you are creating. When you intend to do something, you may or may not have a clear picture of the end-product or the goal. Clarity of intent in one sense is a picture of where you are going or the process you want to experience in getting there. You may simply want to create a happy life, or to be clear in your intent to get something done.

After clarity of intent comes clarity of motivation. What is your motivation for doing something? Whatever action you take, you will want to be clear on why you are doing it. What do you see as the gain? What do you want out of it? A lack of clarity is often perceived after an action is taken, and what is gained is not what is expected. You may have created something you thought you wanted in your life and found it was not what you wanted. If you had been clear about what you wanted, about what you expected to gain, it would have been easier for the universe to bring it to you in many different forms.

There is also clarity of agreement. On every level of personal and interpersonal relationships, in every business relationship, business venture, and group, there are unspoken agreements. The more those unspoken agreements can be spoken, the clearer you will be. Many disappointments and problems occur when agreements are not clear, when one person follows one set of agreements, and the other follows another. Both can be operating from clarity, but if they are not communicating, there can be confusion.

Careful communication
brings clarity.

Clarity of communication means being precise and accurate as you speak. It means not exaggerating your experience, making bad things worse, making good things glamorous. There can be a tendency to exaggerate bad times, and this creates an imprecise communication to the self and others. It creates unfocused, even negative experiences. Watch your words when you speak to others. Are you reflecting accurately your experience, or are you communicating to impress, dazzle, or gain sympathy and understanding? Be clear on what you want to gain when you speak to others. Are you hoping the other person will give you certain things?

Are you operating from many unspoken agreements? It is important to communicate what you expect clearly if you do not want to be disappointed. Communication is one area that controls the life you live and the forms you attract. When you speak precisely and clearly, when you know the intent of your communication, you will find your experience of others and the world changing.

Get clear on your purpose, intent, and motivation.

When you are clear on your purpose, your intent, your motivation, your agreements, when you are clear on your communications, action flows. Many of you want to start with clarity of action, and yet it is clarity of purpose that is the starting point. Clarity of perception lets you create the vision that matches your motivation, inner self and core being.

Clarity in a spiritual sense is an alignment of the physical, mental, and emotional bodies with the spiritual self. It can be accomplished through various techniques. The aura can be cleared by techniques of energy balancing, so that you can work on clarity with your mind. The mind is one of your most powerful tools. You can create clarity through visualizing and working on your aura. Linking the spirit to the mind can bring more clarity than any other step. If you want clarity, ask your soul to give it to you. The spirit has the answers, and a connection to the flows of energy in the earth plane that will bring you abundance, love and peace, and anything else you are asking for.

Think now of something you want clarity on. Imagine that you are going upward into your spirit. Picture it as a fine, light energy. See it flowing through to your mind, literally cleaning house, rearranging your thoughts into a pattern that allows you to become a part of a probable future that is more light and joyful. Feel the energy coming all the way down through your body until all of your bodies—mental, emotional and physical—are aligned. If you want to know more about your life purpose, or about any personal situation, then ask. You will need to create the intention and a time to hear. Take the time to sit quietly. It may not happen the first time you try. But if you continue to create the space for the ideas to come through, that is all that is required.

Any time you create a clear, relaxed space, calm down your mind, and ask for information, you will be given it. Like a radio receiving station, the more you create the space to receive, the more you will receive. The more you spend time getting clear—quiet thinking time, linking up with the higher energies within you—the more you will find yourself taking actions that are entirely different from what you would have done. You may eliminate 80 percent or more of the actions you would have taken. One half-hour spent thinking and getting clear can keep you from spending years on a slower path. You can evolve rapidly on a spiritual level by spending the time to get clear, asking for what you want, and opening to receive it.

PLAYSHEET

1 | Write down something you feel ambivalent or con-
fused about and would like new understanding
and clarity about.

2 | Close your eyes and let a symbol emerge that repre-
sents the highest resolution of this problem. Draw
or describe the symbol here.

3 | Imagine you are placing this symbol upon your heart; ask for clarity and understanding.

A. What insights are you receiving about how to act or think?

B. What beliefs do you have about the outcome? Do these need to be changed to a higher view?

C. What choices do you have? Think of at least three.

D. What do you now *intend* to do?

XV

Freedom is
Your Birthright

Freedom is an inner feeling. It is the ability to choose what you want. It is the knowledge that *you* are the captain of the ship. Freedom is knowing that you own your own life, that you are the one in charge. Freedom is essential for joy, for anywhere you feel trapped or that your rights have been taken away, you cannot experience joy.

Freedom is important if you are to bring the light of your soul into consciousness. You live on a planet of free will, where you learn about action and reaction, cause and effect. Earth reality is based on choice. No matter what situation you are experiencing in your life, whether you *think* you have freedom or not, you have made a choice to be in that situation.

You learn by trial and error. Do not make yourself or others wrong for the choices they make, for you are always growing through the reactions and effects of your actions. In this earth school of free will you call life there are many lessons and challenges of freedom.

The only limits to freedom are those you place upon yourself.

How do you lose your sense of joyous freedom, your birthright of choice? As a small child there are many demands and expectations of you, yet a child has more freedom than it might appear. A child is free to respond in new ways, to learn and to grow without preconceived ideas. A child is free to examine things afresh, to take each experience for what it is and not categorize or analyze based on past experience. A child is free, particularly in the earlier years of life, to form opinions based not on past ideas, but on natural reactions.

As a child grows, some feelings of freedom become lost in the process of developing the mind. The mind begins to look for patterns; it begins to see associations and starts connecting things that would be better understood as independent events. When something happens, the mind begins to look at all other things of a similar nature, often exaggerating the negative by comparing the situation to memories of the past.

As a child, you make strong decisions. A woman who often felt afraid to stand by her creative work discovered that when she was a young child someone had ridiculed a picture she had painted. She became afraid to show people her creative work. She began to hide her drawings, and eventually felt bad about every creative effort. She became afraid to assert her power. She identified new experiences with the old one and in this way froze the degree of choice available in new, but similar circumstances. This led to a loss of freedom—she was no longer free to choose her response to her own power and creativity.

Children make constant and ongoing decisions about the nature of reality. Another woman found it difficult to speak out about things she really believed in. She discovered that as a small child, when making a cake with her aunt, she had been sharply rebuked for a comment she made. She made a decision at that moment—that to be loveable, she needed to keep her opinions to herself. In future situations she operated on that premise. It took away her freedom to respond spontaneously and to see each situation as a new experience. She became afraid to speak up, and found herself intimidated when it came to voicing an opinion that might be challenged.

Freedom is your birthright. It belongs to everyone. Now you may say, I am not free in this or that area of my life. I am not free to quit my job, travel the world, or do what I want. You are free—to the degree you believe yourself to be free.

> To create more freedom in your life,
> do not look at the areas in
> which you do not have freedom;
> look instead at the areas
> where you have created freedom.

Perhaps you have the freedom to stay out late if you want, or the freedom to buy whatever food you want at the grocery store. To have more freedom look at what freedom you already claim as your right. Feeling sorry for yourself for lacking freedom puts you in the role of a victim. Whenever you experience yourself in that role, you are not powerful. Look instead at the areas in which you have chosen not to be the victim of another person or a circumstance. All of you have created freedom in many areas of your life. You can see that you have given yourself many freedoms, freedoms you value greatly and would allow no one to take away.

How about those areas in your life where people are demanding more from you than you want to give? They may want more time, energy, love, or more attention. They may demand it in such a way that you feel a loss of freedom. If this is occurring in your life, try asking yourself if a part of you wants more time and more attention from another part of you than you are willing to give. Anything that you feel another person is taking away from you is symbolic of something you are taking from yourself. If you feel people want more attention than you can give them, or put demands upon you that you cannot and do not choose to meet, ask, "Is a part of me putting demands that can't be met on another part?"

Other people act as mirrors to show you something about what you are doing to yourself. In this case you can ask, "Am I in some way taking something away from myself, not paying enough attention to my own needs?" You can begin by looking at what those needs are and deciding you will pay attention to them. In one case, a man felt his girlfriend was demanding far too much from him in the way of time and space. He enjoyed his many hours spent working alone, and her need for companionship was far greater than his. As he began to examine the demands she put upon him for more attention, he realized that in all of his long hours of work he was not paying attention to himself and his own greater needs. He discovered he was not paying attention to his higher self which was wanting sleep and rest and more attention. He was instead working long, hard hours, ignoring his physical needs and the needs of other parts of himself.

The woman who felt she was not being given the attention and the time she wanted from this man began to look at this as an inner message. She felt they did not play or spend quality time together. On deeper reflection, she realized that she was not giving herself quality time, that she was rushing around all day, responding to the needs of others, and that she was not allowing herself to play and have fun. Everything she blamed her partner for withholding from her was something she was not giving herself.

Freedom is something you create for yourself. It is not given to you and it cannot be taken away. You can choose to give it away and you can choose not to claim it, but others cannot take it. Only you can give it away. There are many areas of freedom in your life you know *nobody* would be able to take away from you. Perhaps you have a favorite place to eat and you feel free to eat there. You know deep inside that no one would be able to stop you. Perhaps you have the freedom to watch a favorite show on TV, and you know no one will stop you. You may notice in these situations that nobody does try to stop you.

When you put out a definite and clear message to the Universe, you rarely have to fight for what you want.

Have you ever rehearsed something in advance, gotten very clear about what you wanted, and then discovered you didn't even need to ask? Struggling to get what you want most often happens when you are not certain you deserve to have it.

Many of you who work feel that you are not free, that in some way or another between the hours of nine and five you have given up your freedom. Freedom is an attitude. To experience freedom in this situation, it may be necessary to look at the larger picture. Why are you in this job? If it is for the money, remember that you freely chose this job to make money and that you are free at any time to find another way to make money. You can create a sense of freedom from moment to moment by realizing you are free to respond, act and feel any way you choose. You are free to speak and take action within the framework of your job. There is always a level of freedom in everything you do. Look at where you are free. Focus on that freedom, and it will increase in your life.

The greatest barrier to freedom lies in the way you think of the world. Lack of freedom does not come from other people, but from your own thinking processes. Many of you take away your freedom by not allowing yourselves a choice of how to react to a given situation. For instance, say your friend always criticizes you, and you always respond with hurt or anger. You can gain freedom by finding new ways to react. Perhaps you can say, "Oh, this friend of mine simply does not know a better way to act." Or, "Perhaps this friend of mine is very critical of himself and he is only criticizing me because it is the way that he talks to himself." You can choose to come from compassion and not take it personally. You can choose to remain centered and balanced even when others around you are not. This is the ultimate freedom, the freedom to choose how you will respond and be, the freedom to act in a way that elevates your energy.

Most people respond in habitual ways, rather than examining their responses. Realize that you can choose how you react and respond to everything in the universe. When some people have deadlines they begin to hurry, rushing everything in their lives. Other people respond by procrastinating and finishing at the last moment. Others respond with depression, feeling that the task is overwhelming, their inner voice telling them they can never do it. You are free to choose—do you want to react to something in a way that makes you feel unhappy or bad about yourself, or react in a way that promotes your self-worth and self-esteem?

Other people respond to you in whatever way their programs and beliefs dictate. Power comes in knowing that you have a choice. You do not need to change other people; you can change your reaction to them. When you choose to feel good you are not dependent on other people acting in certain ways to make you feel good. Before you can attract people who will support, appreciate and acknowledge you, you must choose to do that for yourself.

The degree to which you support and acknowledge yourself will be the degree to which you receive support.

Each time you choose to feel good about yourself, even when someone is criticizing you, putting you down, or acting in a way that you used to respond to with pain, you are choosing joy. Each time you do so you create freedom in your life. You are free from having to have other people act in certain ways for you to be happy. You are free from your own expectations.

Frequently a feeling of pain comes from getting caught in details rather than seeing the larger picture. For instance, a woman became very disappointed in her boyfriend when he did not bring her flowers. She had the picture in her mind that being given flowers meant she was loved. Every time she thought about him not bringing flowers, she felt pain. She was not free to choose joy because of her own internal pictures. When she began to look at the truth and the larger picture, she realized that this man loved her deeply, was very committed to her and did not view giving flowers as a statement of love. As she looked at all the good things that existed between them, she realized she was getting caught in her own expectations; she was choosing pain out of habit.

To *have freedom be willing to give freedom.*

You cannot own another person, nor can you have a relationship of equality when you are taking freedom away from someone else. All people have the right to do what is enlivening and growth-oriented for them. Many people have to leave relationships because they are not given the freedom they need to grow. Some are threatened by the need for freedom in their partner or mate. They interpret a request for freedom as pushing away from them, rather than others' attempts to seek out their own higher selves.

Ironically, the more freedom you give people the more they will want to be with you. Do you demand things of others that you would not want them to demand of you? Do you expect them to report in to you, live up to your pictures, and be there whenever you want? Whatever degree of freedom you take from others is the degree of freedom you take from yourself.

Imagine a prisoner sitting in a cell with a guard who must guard him twenty-four hours a day. The question is, who is really the prisoner, the guard or the prisoner? If you feel that you must watch over others all the time, that you cannot trust them or give them freedom, you are just as much in a trap as they are. Many of you lose your freedom because you are so closely guarding those things that you do not want to have taken away from you. You may guard your mate, your possessions, your children or family in such a way that you are spending more time protecting them than seeking your own growth.

If you experience jealousy, it is often based on a fear that others are giving something to someone else that they are not giving to you. If you look and examine the issue, it is usually something you are not giving yourself. If you are jealous of your mate giving attention to another person and you want to curtail his freedom so that he cannot do so, look again. It may be that your higher self is not being given the attention it is requiring.

Jealousy takes away the freedom of both the one who is jealous and the one who is possessed. If you give yourself what you need—be it attention, love, or something else—then you will not experience jealousy. You will find that you can get satisfaction from many sources, not just from the one you love. Jealousy implies scarcity, that there is not enough. Freedom implies abundance, that there is enough.

Determine now that you will give freedom to everyone close to you.

Let them make their own mistakes and discover their own joys. I can guarantee that anytime you give freedom to others, they will turn to you with even greater love and respect. It takes a centered, balanced and secure person to give others their freedom. It is a great gift to them and to yourself, for the prisoner no longer needs to be guarded and thus the jailer is also free.

You are free when you can choose how you want to respond. If you can choose to react with joy and pleasure, if you can choose to react by seeing the positive, making yourself right rather than wrong, then you have gained the ultimate freedom, the freedom to be and act in a way that reflects your deeper truth.

PLAYSHEET

1 | List at least three areas in which you allow yourself freedom.

2 | Are there any areas in your life you do *not* feel free? Example: I am not free to go back to school.

3 | Do you think it's possible that you could have freedom in those areas of your life? If it's possible, give yourself permission to have freedom in those areas. It may take a while for that freedom to appear in your daily life, but freedom must start with the thought of it. Turn every statement above into a positive affirmation in those areas you feel freedom is possible. Example: I am now free to go back to school.

XVI

Embracing the New

Being open to accept new things, ideas, and people into your life creates an ever expanding capacity for joy. There is a mass thoughtform that the future might be worse than the present. This creates the need to hang on to what you have, freeze things as they are, and keep them from changing. It leads to much pain.

Embracing the new means being open to having more in your life. Many of you think that what you have created up until now is the best you can do. You make something and think that the first try is your best. But on the second and third tries you may do even better. As you create things in your life, you become better and more skilled. That is the process of life. A child who first begins walking is wobbly and unsteady. As the child practices she becomes strong and steady in her stride. It is the same with everything you do, for life is like a spiral in which you circle around again and again, often to the same issues, but each time from a higher perspective.

Opening to new things means trusting and having faith in yourself and others. It means believing that the future holds joy and promise. It means believing in your growth and direction. The heart is the center of faith, trust and belief. Opening to the new means opening your heart. Be willing to step outside of your normal limits and viewpoints and see the world in different ways. Trust that the world is safe and know that you are the director and the producer of what occurs in your life.

Opening to the new takes a willingness to view the old not with hate or anger or disgust, but with compassion. Many of you leave a relationship in anger, or you buy a new car when you are mad at your old one. That is one way to leave the old and embrace the new. As you follow the path of joy you can learn to open to new things while you are in a state of acceptance and peace with the old.

When things are not going well in your life, sometimes you gather the motivation and energy to change them by becoming angry or choosing pain. It need not be difficult to leave the old and embrace the new. If you start thinking of what you want, how you would like your life to be, you begin easily and automatically to draw the new to yourself. If you want something and it can only come when another person changes or acts differently, then you do not have power or control over that. The only power or control you have is over your own emotions and reactions.

*If you want something new,
be open to having it come
from anywhere, any place, any person.*

Be open to surprises and new things. Keep your heart open. Some of you experience a feeling of vulnerability or fear when you think of bringing new people or new things into your lives. What you call tension or anxiety before an event can be viewed instead as focusing your energy to prepare you for something new. It is a change in your vibration to prepare you for something that is finer and higher in your life. You may feel that you must first conquer fear and anxiety before you step out and accomplish something. But everyone has that inner feeling of tension to some degree before attempting new things; it is a period of gathering energy to make the shift into a higher vibration.

Every single thing that happens to you happens to assist you in bringing yourself to a higher level of evolution. Even those things you call negative or bad are there to show you new ways of responding so that you may be more powerful in the future. If it looks like the same problem or a situation is occurring over and over, be aware that every single time it is happening in a new way. Embrace what is new about that pattern or situation and look at how you have succeeded in bringing it to a higher level. Perhaps you are more aware of it than before, or able to understand it better. You may be less emotionally involved and more able to observe the pattern. Every day brings with it new circumstances, challenges and things that allow you the opportunity to grow.

An attitude of openness and receptivity will draw to you many good things. Let go of the fear that the future may mean having less than you have now or may take something away from you. Open up to the idea that you will be wiser, stronger and more powerful tomorrow and that whatever you create will be even better than what you already have. Be open to new concepts and words. They are often the way the universe brings you the signs and guideposts of your next step.

Opening to the new can be experienced in many ways. Many of you have a need for aliveness, excitement and adventure. Often you blame your partner because life seems dull and routine or you blame your job for its monotony. You *can* create that sense of aliveness in everything you do, and you can do it in simple ways. Change your morning routine, get up earlier, go to bed later, change what you do when you get home from work. Even minor changes can stimulate a sense of aliveness.

Every time you
embrace something new,
you bring into yourself
a sense of aliveness.

Your heart expands, and you literally begin revitalizing yourself and rejuvenating your body. Life always seeks growth, expansion and evolution. In experiencing the new you can see more of who you are. You do not need to make the old ways wrong; rather create newness in the old. Only when you do not see the new in the old does growth cease and relationships become dull. You may have seen people who have been to-gether for many years and who act vibrant and young and in love. If you examine the relationship, you will discover that they are doing new things, creating new projects and bringing a sense of aliveness into their personal lives. They are probably conquering new territory, opening to adventure and feeling alive individually, in whatever way is appropriate to them. People who have been together for a long period of time often take each other for granted, going to bed at the same time every night, getting up and going to the same job, doing the same things on the weekend. All of that leads to a sense of contraction around the heart and a sense of boredom and deadness inside.

Opening to the new is a way of youthening your body, of expanding your childlike sense of wonder and awe. As they grow older many people constrict their boundaries; they begin to seek what is comfortable, familiar, and safe. Their world becomes narrow and limited. Life becomes a matter of focusing on the petty rather than focusing on the great. You have seen those people whose concerns are so minor you do not take them seriously. They have ceased to expand into the greater picture of their lives.

There is a new you every day.

Every morning when you wake up you are literally being born anew and afresh. Every day there are new things on your mind, people to meet, things to do. As you wake up and start your day, you need not think of the past and remember mistakes; instead focus upon the future and what you will create.

Try new routines each day; see if you can make even the small things more conscious. When you do new things you are conscious and aware of the present moment. You are paying attention, fully alert. Doing new things is invigorating to the physical body.

You must be able to put many things on automatic to live. Your breathing and many of your bodily functions are automatically controlled. As a child your nervous system develops in such a way that it learns to select information, for if too much information is coming in, there is a lack of focus. So, in the development of your being, there is a learned balance between focusing upon those things that need to be paid attention to, and learning not to be sidetracked by meaningless, trivial and constant data. As a child you developed selective awareness, tuning out many things in your universe so that you could tune in to others.

You have been given the ability to put many things on automatic, making them routine or habitual so you can focus on those things which are truly important. However, because of this ability, many of you react automatically to those things which should be examined. Many of the things you take for granted create discomfort and a lack of well-being.

When you attempt new things, you begin to reexamine all of the habitual and routine things you took for granted. Many people choose jobs that involve danger or tension so they can experience the awareness and attention required to stay alive. They must live in the present moment. Race car drivers, mountain climbers, people who put themselves in positions in which their attention must be focused and fully alert know this experience of adventure and aliveness. It comes when you are not on automatic, but fully conscious and aware of every action. As you embrace the new you begin to bring into consciousness those things that may have been routine. You begin to experience present-time awareness and to live in the moment.

*Power comes from
living in the present moment,
where you can take
action and create the future.*

So as you embrace the new, remember, things are always going to get better; nothing is taken away unless something better is coming. Every down cycle is followed by a great leap forward. It is easy to embrace the new. Play like a child. You have seen how young children embrace everything as a new experience. It can be easy to open up and embrace the new if you picture it as easy. Keep a picture in your mind that the future is positive and that it will be better than anything you have ever known. As you grow and evolve, what you create will be even more joyous than what you have now.

PLAYSHEET

1 | Think of at least three new things, skills, experiences, you brought into your life last year. As you list them, think of how you felt as you learned them or brought them into your life.

2 | Record here what feelings you had after you opened to these new things:

3 | Now, list at least three new experiences, skills to learn, that you would like to bring into your life next year:

XVII

Taking a
Quantum Leap

New ideas and new forward movements do not always come in the form the mind expects. In picturing the highest for yourself it is important that you use your mind to go upward and outward; let your mind come up with the initial images of what you want. As the mind creates pictures, those images go to the light of the soul, to the inner being which creates those pictures. The soul then gives the mind new ideas and visions. It may seem at times that you think of what you want, and by the time you get it, it is different from what you originally asked for. This is because the mind, when requesting something, automatically activates the resources of the greater self. When the request comes back, it comes back in its higher form.

You may have wondered why some of the things you asked for took a long time to come. Quantum leaps involve time and your ability to manifest things. If you went back and looked at what you asked for in the past, you would see that many of the things you did not get, you no longer want, and the things that were for your higher good, you have. Some things you may be preparing to have will come at a later time.

Another level that you operate from, besides the mind, is the spirit. The spirit tells you how to get things not through the mind, but through coincidences, feelings and emotions. After you use your mind to tell the Universe what you want, begin to listen to your spontaneous and creative urges. They may seem to have no relationship to the goal you want to reach. It may seem as if, for instance, you put out for great financial success, and all of a sudden you want to take the summer off and study something else. As you trust your inner urges and study something else, you may find new ideas emerging that bring you the wealth you wanted. The soul is always telling you the right way to go, but you will need to take the leap of faith and trust, and act upon that inner guidance.

*If you are going for
a major change in your life,
you will want to change
those beliefs that kept you
from having it in the past.*

If you are very clear on your intent to get from one place to another, for instance from one level of financial prosperity to another, or one level of creative success to another, then there will be changes that you must undergo in yourself. Because, if you were already there on the various levels of personality and emotions and mind, you would not need to do anything. You would already have what you want. A woman came to me and said, "I want to be a millionaire. Today I cannot pay my rent, but I want to be a millionaire, and I would like to have it as quickly as possible." If she *believed* she could have it, she would already have it at that point.

When you put a request for a quantum leap out to the universe, the request goes upward from your mind to your spirit. The spirit then begins broadcasting signals back to your mind and emotional selves, telling them how to create the changes you want. Now, you must pay attention to those signals. There are many levels at which changes will need to happen for you to achieve this new step. For instance, in our example of greater financial prosperity, that person might need to learn many of the principles of creating money. Therefore, her soul may direct her to read many books or send someone along who can teach and instruct her. It may be that she is not willing to let go of her old images of lack of money. It may be that her heart is not yet open enough to believe that she can receive and deserve that kind of money. So there will be many lessons sent to her to help open her heart. In fact, her level of trust may be so undeveloped that the making of the money may be delayed while she develops faith and trust.

Whatever you ask for, you may have to let go of something to get it. If you have asked for money, you may have to let go of your images of the lack of it, of all of the ways you live that reflect those images, and of the ways you spend and buy. Your soul will give you many challenges and growth opportunities to help you let go of those images of lack. The money may come at first in small amounts so that you can demonstrate your willingness to spend on those things that create prosperity. Eventually as the energy is changed within you, as your programs and decisions and beliefs are rewritten, ideas will begin flowing, concrete ideas about specifically how to create the sum of money you want. It may be a year or two or even more before the programs around lack of abundance are cleared up enough for the specific idea to come in. At that point, you will continue to create many ways to attract wealth and refine them until it is a fact.

Some people stop along the way when something does not come immediately, because their minds cannot see the connection between the lessons that are occurring and their request for a major change. Their minds may even interpret that some of the events are taking them in the wrong direction, and that although they are asking for something over and over, the opposite is occurring. However, if you look at how much you are growing from having the opposite of what you want (or what appears to be), you will see that in fact these events are working on your energy and opening you in certain ways to have what you are asking for.

For instance, one woman asked for an increase of 100 percent in her monthly salary. Shortly thereafter, her boss had to cut her salary in half due to business problems. It looked to her like she was getting the opposite of what she asked for. However, she began to think about starting her own business in a related field, something she had wanted to do for years. The cut in pay became a motivation to move forward and start her own business. She did indeed make the salary she asked for, several years later, in her own business.

As you can see, change is much more involved than simply asking for something and having it. You may need to go inward, expand your faith and trust, and open your heart. You need to trust in your inner guidance and impulses to move from your present level of abundance to a greater one. You also need to let go of many old images about who you are. You will have many growth opportunities offered to you to change those mental images. At the soul level, it is always a joy to grow, and the soul is always concerned that you are growing. Whether you are growing through pain or joy, it is the growth that is the end goal, the growth that is required to have what you have decided you want. The soul lets your mind operate with a great deal of free will in choosing for yourself which goals you will bring about, or what quantum leaps you want.

The higher you can aim with your mind, the more you can join with the growth of your soul. As your mind thinks of new ideas, it goes upward and links with your spirit, which is outside the denser energies of the earth plane. The spirit speaks back to you through your emotions, most frequently through your feelings, by giving you a feeling or an urge of something it wants you to do. When these feelings and urges come through, at that point you sometimes will want to ignore your mind (not make it wrong), for the mind will often look for reasons and explanations before taking action. If you have a strong urge to do something, it is important to follow that urge. Your mind may try to make up reasons why you should or should not follow the urge, for your mind follows the familiar programs it knows. Your urges come from your soul, which has a much broader picture than your mind can conceive of to get you what you want. It leads you in directions your mind cannot anticipate.

So you will want to make a decision, as you take a quantum leap, to follow your inner guidance, the inner urges of your feeling level, of your soul. There are two levels of reality. In one your mind puts out a goal, is very clear in its intent, makes the decision to have it, and commits your will. The second level is the soul level; from it the higher self goes out in all directions and magnetizes you to the coincidences, people and events that create what you want. This happens beyond the level of the mind; you must follow your inner urgings and guidance to join this flow.

You can choose
how quickly
you wish it to happen.

To make the time between asking for what you want and receiving it shorter, begin by getting clear on your goals. Some of you are so nonspecific that your minds wander around, never making clear requests to your souls and so your souls spend much time guiding your minds to get clear about what you want. The more accurately and precisely you can state what you want in any area of your life—with exact guidelines and steps— the more rapidly you will have it. You may not get it in the precise form you asked for, but your soul will create for you the essence of what you want.

In being precise, you are formulating essence. Essence is the growth that you are going for in any quantum leap, and I would suggest that you take anything you have requested and ask, "What is the essence of it?" If you look at what you have tried to create, you will see that you have always gotten the essence of everything you asked for. For instance, if you wished for a loving relationship, you may have wanted simply to feel loved. Your soul may give you love in many ways, perhaps through a close friend, child or pet, perhaps through a job promotion, or in any of the ways you accept love. If you want to create a more fit body, the essence you want may be more self-love. If you are willing to go for essence in your quantum leaps, you will be able to create them far more rapidly.

If you are tempted to go back into the past and say, "Well, I wanted this, but I did not get it," look at the core, at the essence, of what you requested. I would say you have gotten it in many ways. The soul is quite creative in interpreting your request. The soul has to be creative, for the mind is fairly narrow in its ability to ask. The soul takes any request for growth and expands it in every direction it can.

There are some agreements between the mind and the soul. One is the agreement that the mind will look for the specific areas for growth to occur in. Meanwhile, the soul expands the pictures and the choices that the mind has. The mind can act upon the soul's opportunities or not. So there is a constant interplay between the soul and the mind, much as there is a dance between mind and body. The mind creates the image of what it wants, and sends the data to the body. The body can accept and act upon the guidance the mind is giving, or it can choose not to.

Emotional changes
are often required
for a quantum leap.

When your emotions are heavy and sad or negative, the aura around your body is dense. It is like driving with a dirty windshield. You cannot see clearly or far. The light of your soul does not come through brightly. Your soul will guide you to look at those areas in your life that are creating emotional disturbance and stop reacting to them. Find ways to calm your emotions, for calm emotions speed up the time it takes to reach your goals. When you are calm, and peaceful, your soul comes through your emotions to give you that inner guidance. The soul gives guidance through the emotional body, in urges, insights, and those sudden feelings that take you into new arenas.

Taking a quantum leap does not mean searching for relief from worry or disappointment, but creating delight and joy. Look back at those times in which you did something great and you will see the motivation of desire that led you to create it. Often you say, "I *should* do this, or create this or that, to make me happy." If doing those things only brings you a sense of relief, you will probably continue to make it a *should* and not an accomplished fact. You must find desire-motivation for those things you want to do. You need great motivation and a real inner drive to make a quantum leap. It will not work if it is only something your mind has created as a nice thing to do, or something that might feel good. It needs to be something that you can get behind at all levels, that your emotions can feel excited about, something that you truly want to do.

Disliking poverty, for instance, is not enough to get you out of it. You need to truly desire and love to make money if you want to have it. You cannot get what you want by hating your lack of it. So ask, when you look at the quantum leap you want to make, what *is* your motivation? If you see that there isn't any motivation other than to relieve you of feeling bad about who you are, ask "What can I create as a motivation?" Those things you create and go towards are things you feel highly charged about, that bring you great joy and delight. You can always find the money for something you want to do. You can always find the time for something that excites you. And it is the same for taking a quantum leap. If you have an area in which you think you *should* make a big change but you haven't done it yet, ask if you really intend to do it. You know the difference.

If you are working towards quantum leaps that have not yet occurred, be aware that everything you are doing right now in your life is getting you closer. Go inward for a moment and ask "What quantum leap am I in the process of taking? And how could something that happened in the last week or even today be preparing me to have it?"

The mind works better if it has fixed reference points in its progress along the way.

In some ways the mind is like a child. Children do not want to think of high school when they are two years old. They want to think of food, or their friends. The mind is the same way. Create something that is delightful tomorrow—one small step, or one small point of action that will bring you one step closer to your goal. The mind likes to have markers and feel a sense of accomplishment. What would be delightful for you to create tomorrow that would bring you one step closer to your higher goal? At the same time ask your-self, "Is there any inner urging that I have right now about something I want to do that I have been putting off?" Something you have been thinking might take too much time, or might be off course?

In these ways you can begin working with your emo-tions and your mind to bring a quantum leap even closer. If each day you wake up and say, "What is my inner urging today?" and ask "What can I create so that my mind can see I am taking action to get closer to my goal?" there will be much greater progress in your leap forward. The mind likes to have a sense that it has ac-complished things; you must keep it satisfied. The emotions are also much happier when they can see pro-gress. Be aware that the actual steps you take may not turn out to be the necessary ones. They can still be quite satisfying and bring a sense of forward move-ment. The mind is unable at times to connect what is going on—the phone calls, the particular problems that come up—with forward movement. Often you have a great picture or vision, but each little piece of the puz-zle is happening in present time and may not seem to fit the whole. Even a comment a friend makes to you, or a phone call, can very much be part of your forward movement. The mind, not knowing all of the areas that are being opened, or all the beliefs that are being changed, often cannot see the pattern and the move-ment. It does not think you are growing or that your goal is being reached. If it becomes impatient or disbe-lieving, it can cloud your emotions and make the leap more difficult. If you can give your mind the satisfac-tion of having accomplished an action, it should also help your emotions.

Ask yourself what step would you like to take that would be a step towards your goal. Ask yourself if there are any inner urges you have been getting for something you could do in the next month. It need not even seem related to your goal.

Make the decision that you will do it.

TAKING A QUANTUM LEAP
PLAYSHEET

1 | What quantum leap would you like in your life?

2 | Is there anything you would have to let go of to have it (belief, attitude, thing, person)?

3 | What is the essence of this goal? Is there any other form that will give you the essence of what you want?

4 | What is your motivation to have it, i.e. what would you get out of it?

5 | Often, inner urges or whispers in your mind are connected to your quantum leap, even though they may not appear to be related. List any inner urges you have been having here.

6 | What specific step, no matter how simple, can you take in the next week towards your goal?

XVIII

Living in
Higher Purpose

Higher purpose is a stream of energy you join when you create something that serves mankind or your own spiritual evolution. Without higher purpose you are a wanderer, roaming around, taking various paths with many potential wrong turns and lost time. With higher purpose, you can choose every moment, knowing what to do with the hour, the day, and the week. It allows you to grow and evolve rapidly in this lifetime.

Everyone on earth has a higher purpose. You came to earth to be a part of a system of energy that deals with emotions, personality, and thoughts, that involves seeing what is inside of you reflected in the outside world. You did this so you could create and see around you who you are. There are other universes in which forms come and go more quickly; almost the minute they are thought of, they appear and disappear.

Things move more slowly here. Time is literally

slowed down so you can focus on certain things. You segmented yourself into a certain time frame called birth to death, and are working on specific energies. I am speaking of the larger framework of the universe, for on a universe scale, the earth plane is very slow. The wave of the note is very long, so that you can experience matter. From that perspective, you want to evolve upward to the highest frequency of this note, so you may go on to other places where the rules change. There are places where you are more a pure energy being, unbound by the concrete world of time, space and matter.

Here your thoughts create and become reality; it could be said yours is a world of frozen thought. It takes longer to create form, and for some of you, even longer to let it go. Because time on this plane is slow, you must practice economy of energy, and that is one of the reasons it may seem to take so long to create what you want.

If you focus on having something, you can go straight to it with purpose. It may still be a matter of years before you reach your goals, for you who are authors, or into physical training, but having a higher purpose saves time. When I speak of higher purpose, I am speaking of compacting time, speeding up the evolution of your soul, and raising your vibration. The more you have a purpose, the less you waste energy, and the faster you can go higher. Ultimately, higher purpose is spiritual evolution.

The new home, the finished book is not the goal of growth. But the process by which you create these things and the growth it gives you—the new skills you acquire, the insights, the opening of your heart when you love, the new appreciation for beauty your garden gives you when the flowers come up, the feelings that you have when you finish a project, the focus and concentration when you work—this is higher purpose, this is evolution.

Spiritual growth means increasing your awareness of beauty, opening your heart, and experiencing more love and compassion.

When I speak of higher purpose, I am speaking of soul-purpose, which is to balance all your energies, and harmonize your being with your soul's note. Each one of you has a soul sound, a note; and the more you can express it outward into the world through your voice, the more you can create forms in the outer world that match your inner being. You will notice that as you sound your note, you begin breathing more deeply and rhythmically. You can start by letting sounds come out of your mouth, until you find a beautiful, comfortable sound. This will assist you in clearing your aura and raising your vibration, just to sound beautiful, comfortable notes. It will harmonize the various parts of your being.

There are many ways in which evolution occurs, depending on where you are on your path. Ultimately, souls start out on earth in the denser energies, and work their way up into the higher and finer energies. Some of you do it very quickly, and others of you take longer. What are some of the things that make it take longer to grow? One is the inability to let go of form when there is no essence behind it. When a form has been created, but the reason for the form is gone, then it is time to let it go. You have seen this in relationships, how many hang on to the shell of it when the life energy is out of the connection. Another thing that slows your evolution is lack of purpose. If you are looking upward, intending to go higher, then you will, if that is your purpose. You can then take every situation in your life and ask, "Does this evolve and bring me higher, or does it not?" And if it does not, you can ask again, "Is there any way I can change this situation or be with this person in such a way that I can grow?"

Any situation you are in can be spent in higher purpose. You can come out of the denser energies of heavy emotions, fear or pain. The earth plane can be a beautiful place to experience. The ability to enjoy the senses, to hear sounds, touch, feel, and know love can be joyous experiences. You *can* come out of separateness. In so many ways you create separateness and loneliness. In your universe you not only have individual bodies, but you are so often separated from your own deep self. For instance, every time you have a doubt, thinking you are not good or strong enough, you have separated from your higher self. The path of your soul is to join together all your parts and merge with your higher self.

You can also talk of purpose in terms of the concrete things you wish to accomplish. I would recommend first that you ask, "What is the essence behind the form?" For instance, if you want to start a business, what is its highest purpose, how does it serve the planet? How does it serve you? If you want to reach a financial goal, you can first ask, what is the essence of that goal? How do I serve my higher purpose by creating that form? If you want money to get your work out into the world, to create a project that will heal others, if you want simply to be a vehicle for it (not for egotistical reasons), then the universe will send you money in abundance. But anything you seek to possess or hold onto will slow down your growth. The universe, in its loving, gentle way, will seek to prevent you from having it. If you are allowed to have those things you hang onto long after they are of use to you, you will find yourself living in a harder, heavier energy, one of more struggle.

Life need not be hard.

You can create joy by softening your energy. What do I mean by softening it? Whenever people are mad at you, you can easily respond with anger and hardness. Or you can soften so much that you look at them with deep compassion. This separates your energy from theirs at the personality level, and connects you in the heart.

Many of you think that you need to have great will and control over your energy. If you are living with purpose, you will find you are also living in harmony with your energy, not needing to control it. On a concrete level, this means not spending idle time, even in your mind, and resisting the temptation to go over past situations that did not bring you joy. Again, sounding your note, singing, is a way to bring yourself back to center. Notice your mind becoming clearer and freer when you do so. The more you sound your note, the more you will find one that feels in harmony with your being. It is not something that can be taught, but something that you must find for yourself. It is a joyful, comfortable, peaceful sound, and you always feel better afterwards.

Before you were born, you did not decide *how,* you simply decided what energies you would evolve within yourself. The things that happen, the careers you choose, the people you attract are simply the effect of your evolution. They are the creation and the product of it. You may be confused, thinking that a new house, or person, marks your progress. In one way they do, but your progress has already been made, long before they came.

Go inward for a moment, feel your energy, and allow a picture, symbol, image, feeling, or word to come which represents your purpose here. What is your growth centering around in this lifetime? What have been your main challenges? What, in form, have you been wanting to create in your outer world?

Higher *purpose is always something you love.*

In the next month, become more aware of your purpose. It is always playful and joyful. Higher purpose leads to the finer energies of life, such as a deep connection with a loved one, the joyful union of friends as they play, focus and lightness as you carry out your life work. Joy can exist in every moment if you are willing to live in purpose.

Manifesting higher purpose means believing in yourself, and believing in the goodness of the universe. If you were to make one decision that would assist you most in manifesting higher purpose, it would be to believe in yourself and to trust the universe. From my perspective, there is so much love, there are so many people within five miles of your home you could connect with in a loving way, there is such an abundance of money in your society, that any purpose you decide upon can be created.

How would it feel if every cell of you acknowledged and was in touch with your higher purpose? Holding that purpose in your heart, you would refine your physical body, raise your thoughts upward and bring peace to your emotions. The process of purpose is reaching into your inner self, bringing it out to the world, and going upward with your energy. This life gives you an opportunity to find light, and to live joyfully. Whatever you achieve by the time you die is yours. Every gain you make, every place in your life you insert joy, every place you find laughter, peace, and delight, will already be there for the next lifetime, wherever you may be. Every time you evolve your body, eat in a better way, exercise more, dance, play, focus, bring in light, you evolve in future lifetimes also. Part of the purpose of earth life is to bring in your higher self and join with your spirit at all levels. Each one of you has the ability to help and heal others, and most of you have a sincere desire to do so.

Wake up in the morning even once a year and hold your higher purpose in your hands as a symbol. Do the process I spoke of: Imagine that you are holding in your hands the highest purpose you came to create in this lifetime. Bring it into your heart. Pour light into it, ask for guidance and assistance from the higher forces. Feel your energy going upward and let go of it so that it may come back to you. You will send out a call to the universe telling it you are willing to grow. You will then be given many opportunities to expand and evolve, and none of your challenges will ever be beyond that which you the have skills and tools to handle. Earth can be a very gentle place. However, in some of the coarser and denser levels of energy, it may not feel so gentle.

*You learn and grow
from everything you create.*

You create crisis because it is a time in which you are close to your soul, in which you reach inward, outward, and upward and connect with your purpose. If you are willing to live in higher purpose, listen to yourself and connect with your soul, taking action on its whispers, you will not have to create crisis or struggle. You do not even need to know the form of your purpose, but only have the intent to create higher purpose to bring it to you. Purpose represents movement of the soul, the energy that connects heaven and earth. It is marked by concrete forms—a new house, a marriage, those things that you have been seeking. But those are only the ceremonies that mark new growth in the soul. Because you are growing, all of you, so rapidly, you must create new challenges to experience who you are. These can be joyful opportunities in the higher realms, or crisis and struggle in the lower realms.

If you want to live in higher purpose, begin making it more of a commitment. How do you spend your time? Where do your thoughts go when you are alone? Learn to hold a higher focus, to spend time, when you have nothing better to do, thinking of why you are here and what you have to offer mankind. Purpose comes through serving the higher self, assisting others, and being willing to carry out whatever your vision is of the highest service you can offer. Think of something you can do next week, something specific that you would know to be part of your higher purpose, be it your short-term or long-term purpose. Affirm that you will be willing to acknowledge when you have done or created this, that you are living in higher purpose. When you complete it, you can create one more new concrete thing to do, building the stepping stones to living in purpose.

Tomorrow, as you go through your day, tell yourself what a beautiful person you are. See the beauty in yourself. Feel your inner strength, acknowledge how good you are. Recognize how loving you are, and sense the light around you. Acknowledge yourself, and as you do so, look for your higher purpose. You know what you want to do next. You may have reasons why you cannot do it, old memories and patterns that seem to stop you, but you do know what you want. Bring it up to the surface, pull it up from the unconscious, from the whispers in your mind, and make it real. Hold your vision in front of you. If you want a peaceful and quiet life, to be a good parent, to have a man or woman in your life who loves and values and treasures you, bring up that vision. Make a decision and you will have it.

Get clear on your intent. If you want to serve the world and get your work out, if you want to create prosperity, to open to new creativity and skills, there is always a part of you that knows how. Talk to that part, ask it to show you what steps to take. Watch your inner dialogue, and listen for messages from this part.

Manifesting is a matter of trusting and believing in yourself, and holding that vision in front of you. There are many reasons to stop believing and trusting in the universe and yourself, but there are also many reasons to continue. You are often tested by the universe to see how much you believe in your vision. Every goal is reachable if you keep working on it.

PLAYSHEET

1 | Think of one specific goal you have right now. Write it here.

2 | Close your eyes and think of a symbol of the highest fulfillment of that goal, which includes its purpose for you and mankind. Draw or describe your symbol here.

3 | Take that symbol into your hands, draw it close to your heart and ask,

    A. How does this goal bring more light into my life?

    B. How does it bring more light into others' lives?

    C. How does it serve mankind?

4 | What one step, however small, could you take today or tomorrow towards this goal?

XIX

Recognizing Life Purpose–
What are you here to do?

Many of you are in a state of transition. States of transition always create much energy. Whether you are feeling high or low, you certainly feel alive, full of spirit and energy, whenever your life is changing. That strong part of you, the part that is able to detach and observe, that is looking at the light, that wants your life to be better, more joyful and more peaceful comes out at these times.

What are you here to do? Recognizing life purpose enables you to manifest your destiny. Do not get me wrong; you are free beings. You did not set out a course before you were born that you *had* to follow. You laid some groundwork, provided yourself with certain parents, and chose to be born in a certain part of the world. You set up circumstances for your life so you would be aimed like a projectile in a certain direction. Once you are here, your life is absolutely spontaneous and decided upon from moment to moment. There is no predetermined limit to how high you can go. There are no limits!

You live in a limitless world;
you can expand beyond
anything you know.

To look at your life purpose, look beyond the mass thoughtforms that exist. Many of you have grown up with a great deal of pressure to do, to accomplish, to be, to make a name for yourselves, to feel worthy in one way or another. When you look at life purpose, ask your soul and your self, "Am I doing this for me, for my highest good, or am I doing it to please others, to live up to their image of me? Am I accomplishing this purpose so that I may receive a pat on the back, or recognition? Or am I doing it because it is something I want to do, that fits who I am, that brings me joy?"

There are so many programs and beliefs I see in your culture about being a good and valuable person—by making a lot of money, or being well known, or being quite pious. All of these things can be good if they are done from the soul's desire. But they can be off your path if they are done only to fulfill an image that comes from the ego or personality. Look at yourself right now and ask, if society had no images it held up and admired as being good or right, what would you do with your life? There has been an emphasis on outer productivity in your culture rather than on inner peace, joy, love, and compassion. There is a sense of *time* that pervades everything—accomplish this or that by the age of such and such, or be a failure. There is a sense of pressure, that everything must be done fast. I will say you have been given all the time you need if you come from life purpose in your actions.

You can relax and know that as you go through each day, you have the time to accomplish your purpose. If you do not feel you are accomplishing your purpose, that you do not have enough time, then I will say that what you are doing is probably not your purpose. When you are creating your life purpose you will have enough time, for you will create the time. You will find it so joyful that everything else falls away, and your determination, focus and your concentration *is* there. If there is anything you are forcing yourself to do out of duty or obligation, out of feeling that people will admire you or respect you when you do it, then you are probably not honoring the light of your soul.

Each one of you has a different purpose, and you cannot judge others by what you see them doing. Each one of you has set out to learn certain things in this lifetime, to grow in every way possible. Many of the blocks to manifesting life purpose come from the cultural mass thoughtforms, a lack of training, and other people, particularly those close to you. In a close personal relationship, people tend to take on the goals and the thoughtforms of the other. As you look at your life purpose, look at who you are close to in your life, and ask, have you been manifesting what they wanted for you? Or are you clear about what you want for yourself? Often those who love you the most can be the ones who most hold you back. Not through their negativity, but through their love, through their wanting you to be there for them, to live up to their pictures and roles.

As you look at your life purpose, ask, what would you do if you were alone? If you did not have anyone in your life who would gain from what you did, or lose from it either, would it change your choices? What would *you* do for yourself? What would bring you peace and joy? What if society did not exist or had absolutely different values—would you still love what you are doing? A hundred years ago, the values in this land were different. People were admired for many things that are no longer valued. Society's beliefs are a changing fluid thing, and if you base your life purpose on what you see around you, then it will be a fluid and changing thing that will not necessarily reflect your soul.

Imagine that you are a rock in a stream and the stream is moving all around you. Now, many of you let the stream carry you this way or that. Do you stay centered and balanced while the current flows by, or do you let every current throw you around?

Imagine you have an antenna in your mind, and you can adjust it right now so that it is aimed upward, to the higher ideals that fit you. What do you value in yourself? How do you want to feel? Stop for one moment and ask, what feelings do I want? How do I want my universe to look right now? On an emotional level, bring those feelings to yourself as if right now at this moment you had your perfect universe. Keep this antenna adjusted upward to higher levels of the universe and you will be stable like the rock, while all the currents flow by you.

It *is only an illusion*
that you do not have
what you want.

If you believe in what you see, then you are believing in the creations of the past. Everything you have right now in your life, you created from the past. Everything you have from here on out can be created at this moment, and it can be created differently. You do not need to know specifically what you will do tomorrow or the next day. You can start by *believing* that you do have a purpose, a concrete purpose, and you can begin by asking it to unfold for you. If you begin believing in and acting as if you know what to do with your life, you will. Get up tomorrow and pretend that you are the captain of your ship, and that for one day you will guide this ship the way you want to. You will take the time you need, be with the people you want to be with, say "no" when you want to say "no," and "yes" when you want to say "yes." You will check in from hour to hour to see if you are feeling joy or peace or whatever you have determined that you want to feel.

Some have said their life purpose is serving and assisting others. This can be a very good and true life purpose if the self is centered, and if you are paying attention to making your own life work. By taking care of *you*, putting yourself in an environment that increases your sense of peace and serenity, beauty and harmony, you are much more in a position to assist others than if you put the focus on making them happy and not on yourself. If every person came from a space of harmony and beauty, of the higher self, you would have an entirely different society. Right now look around at all of your options and your choices. Decide you will, from today onward, create the world that you want. Go within and find that point of strength, that part of you that has always been able to create the things you wanted and feel it growing stronger. The greatest gift you give another is having your own life work.

Life change and transition are often preceded by confusion, by a sense of loss or pain, or by a sense that things are falling apart. That is because there is little training in your society about letting go and detaching from forms that are no longer appropriate. There is a mass thoughtform of scarcity, which makes it even harder to let go, thinking there will be nothing better to replace what you're losing. If you focus on what you want, if you acknowledge that what you have is a creation of the past that can be *easily* changed, your future can look any way you choose.

Fill your thoughts with what you want to create, and you will have it.

There is often a time lag between the new thought and the having of it that confuses and stops many people from continuing to think of the new. Thoughts are real and go outward to create what they think of, and thoughts exist in time. So past thoughts may still affect you for a while, even as you change your thinking. Within two to three months, however, the new thoughts will have gained momentum and will have created new outer forms to match.

Honor yourself as a unique individual. When you are with other people, don't compare your path to theirs. Often you compare what they are doing with their life to what you are doing with yours, and feel better than or less than others. Instead, go inward and look at what your highest path is, and compare your life to that. You read stories in the newspapers about what happened to other people and you may think, "This may happen to me." You do not have their thoughts, you are not them. Whatever happens to others happens because of who they are. If you hear other people's stories, do not bring them into your space and internalize them, but ask yourself, "How can I be true to who I am?" "What is *my* truth?" Every single person has a different path, is a unique expression of life force.

<blockquote>

Life *purpose is whatever path
you decide on,
for all is free will.*

</blockquote>

You set up certain conditions so you would want certain things. You can have what you want, if you are willing to hold up the vision and believe in yourself consistently. The more consistently you believe in yourself, the better the results. It would be easy if there were no setbacks (as you interpret them), or trials along the way. Honor every single setback, every single challenge or difficulty, for it strengthens your purpose. It gives you opportunities to be even more committed to your vision, even clearer on your intent. If life were too easy or simple, most of you would be complaining of boredom. Honor your challenges, for those spaces that you label as dark are actually there to bring you more light, to strengthen you, to firm your resolve, and to bring out the best in you.

PLAYSHEET

1 | Close your eyes and allow a picture, symbol or image to come to mind that represents your purpose here on earth.

2 | Bring your symbol into your heart. Ask the higher forces of the universe to breathe more light and life into it. Draw your symbol here.

3 | Imagine your symbol changing color, texture and size, and let it speak to you with its wisdom and show you how it can be released to help serve mankind.

Companion Books

By Orin

Personal Power Through Awareness
A Guidebook for Sensitive People

This is an accelerated, step-by-step course in sensing energy. Using these easy-to-follow processes, thousands have learned to create immediate and profound changes in their relationships, self-image, and ability to love and be loved. You need no longer be affected by other people's moods or negativity. You can recognize when you have taken on other people's energy and easily release it. You can learn to stay centered and balanced, know who you are, increase the positive energy around you, and help and heal others. Your sensitivity is a gift. Learn to use it to send and receive telepathic messages, increase your intuitive abilities, and open to higher guidance. You can leave the denser energies, where things are often painful, and live in the higher energies where you can feel loving, calm, focused, and positive.

Spiritual Growth
Being Your Higher Self

This book will teach you how to bring your higher self into every part of your life. You will learn how to work with the higher powers of the universe to accelerate your spiritual growth. You will learn how to link with the Higher Will, connect with the Universal Mind to create what your want, open your clairvoyant sight, receive revelations, and see the bigger picture of the universe. You will learn non-attachment, right use of will, and how to lift the veils of illusion. You will learn how to expand and contract time, choose your reality, become transparent, communicate in higher ways, and be your higher self. These tools will help you live your everyday life with more joy, harmony, peace, and love. This book will help you align with the higher energies that are coming, using them to live the best life you can imagine for yourself. (H J Kramer, Inc., available February 1989, 240 pages)

By Orin and DaBen

Opening to Channel
How to Connect With Your Guide
By Sanaya Roman and Duane Packer
Orin and DaBen – a wise and healing spirit teacher channeled by Duane Packer – will teach you how to connect with and verbally channel a high-level guide. Channeling is a skill that can be learned, and Sanaya and Duane have successfully trained thousands to channel using these safe, simple, and effective processes. You will learn what channeling is and how to know if you are ready to channel, go into trance, receive information clearly, what to expect in your first meeting with your guide, and much more. (H J Kramer, Inc., 1987, 264 pages)

Creating Money
Keys to Abundance
By Sanaya Roman and Duane Packer
Orin and DaBen show you how to follow the spiritual laws of money and abundance, use advanced manifesting techniques, and create what you want. You will learn how to discover and draw your life's work to you. This book contains many simple techniques, positive affirmations, and exercises to help you create rapid changes in your prosperity. Abundance is your natural state, and as you use the information in this book you will learn how to let money and abundance flow readily into your life while doing what you love. You can develop unlimited thinking, listen to your inner guidance, and transform your beliefs. Discover how to work with energy to easily create what you want and tap into the unlimited abundance of the universe. (H J Kramer, Inc., 1988, 282 pages)

More from Orin
Audio Cassette Tape Albums

A Message from Orin about these Guided Meditation tapes:

I offer these guided meditations to you who have read my books and want to go further, using and living these principles. Working with guided meditations, where your mind is in a relaxed, open state, is one of the most powerful ways known to create rapid, profound, and lasting changes in your life. Many of you who are drawn to my books are "old" evolved souls, and I have used processes and techniques that I feel are most effective for people at your soul level. I have carefully selected the processes, words, and images on the tapes to awaken you to who you are. These guided meditations contain powerful and effective tools of light to create positive changes in your life. I transmit energy to you directly through my voice. I work with your Higher Self, conscious mind, and subconscious mind for lasting changes. You can create miracles by working with light, energy, thought, and your Higher Self. I offer these meditations to you who want to take a quantum leap, accelerate your growth, and live a life of joy rather than of struggle.   *–Orin*

I offer these *Living With Joy* tape albums for you who want to take the principles in the book *Living With Joy* and put them into practice. They make an excellent home-study course. Or, listen with your friends and use these tapes to conduct your own classes.

Living With Joy Volume I – The Path of Joy, by Orin. Contains inaudible sound frequencies for right/left brain wave synchronization and deep-level meditation. Includes: Finding Your Path of Joy; Changing Negatives into Positives; The Art of Self-Love; Self-Worth & Self-Esteem: Power: Refining Your Ego; Knowing Your Heart's Wisdom; Opening to Receive; and Gratitude and Appreciation. Set of 4 tapes with 8 processes in vinyl cassette album. *(L201) $59.95 (Individual tapes not sold separately.)*

Living With Joy Volume II – Taking a Quantum Leap, by Orin. Contains inaudible sound frequencies for right/left brain wave synchronization and deep-level meditation. Includes: Finding Inner Peace; Balance and Stability; Clarity; Freedom; Embracing the New; Taking a Quantum Leap; Living in Higher Purpose; and Recognizing Life Purpose. Set of 4 tapes with 8 processes in vinyl album. *(L202) $59.95 (Individual tapes not sold separately; free tape offer does not apply to albums.)*

Order *Living With Joy,* Volumes I & II – set of 8 tapes with 16 processes in vinyl album – and save over $19. *(L203) $99.95*

Call or write for a Free Subscription to our Newsletter:

To receive a FREE subscription to our newsletter with messages from Orin about current earth changes, information on the energies present, and how to work with them, as well as information about tapes and seminars write: LuminEssence Productions, P.O. Box 19117, Oakland, CA 94619 or call (415) 482-4560. Be sure to include your name, address, and phone number. This newsletter is Orin's way of continuing to assist you in your spiritual growth. Each newsletter gives you additional tools of light and new playsheets called "Light Play" to assist you in Living With Joy.

Single Tape Guided Meditations by Orin

Living with Joy Affirmations Side 1, Guided Journey Side 2 (L100)
   Based on the book's principles.
Attracting Your Soul-Mate (RE002)   **Opening to Receive** (L106)
Taking a Quantum Leap (L103)   **Reprogramming at Cellular** (SI056)
Discovering Your Life Purpose (L104)   **Lucid Dreaming** (SI024)
Radiating Unconditional Love (P103)   **Self-Love** (L102)
Losing Weight, Looking Younger (SI030)
Clearing Blockages (SI057)   **Achieving Intimacy** (RE005)
Self-Employed: Creating Money, Business, Sales (SI037)
Opening Up Psychic Abilities (013)   **Opening Your Chakras** (016)
Meeting Your Spirit Guide (014)   **Being Your Higher Self** (SI040)
Overcoming the Self-Destruct: Subpersonality Journey (SI060)

All tapes listed above are $9.98 each. Most tapes contain the same journey on both sides, with inaudible sound frequencies added to one side for deeper level meditation. Music by Michael Hammer. Individual tapes are not the same as tapes in *Living With Joy* (L201 and L202) tape albums.

Books by Orin   (Published by H J Kramer, Inc.)

Personal Power Through Awareness, Book II of the Earth Life Series by Orin, 216 pages *(PPTA)* **$10.95**

Spiritual Growth: Being Your Higher Self, Book III of the Earth Life Series by Orin, 240 pages *(SG)* **$10.95**

Opening to Channel: How to Connect with Your Guide, by Sanaya Roman and Duane Packer, an Orin and DaBen book, 264 pages *(OTC)* **$12.95**

Creating Money: Keys to Abundance, by Sanaya Roman and Duane Packer, an Orin and DaBen book, 282 pages *(CM)* **$12.95**

Include postage as per order form; California residents add sales tax.

Audio Cassette Tape Albums

Transformation: Evolving Your Personality. These meditations assist you in handling blockages, doubts, mood swings, old issues coming up, over-stimulation, and things that come from being on an accelerated path of growth. Meditations include: Self-Appreciation; Honoring Your Path of Awakening; Focusing Inward: Hearing Your Soul's Voice; Focusing Upward: Hearing the Voice of the Masters and Guides; Reparenting Yourself; Creating the Future with Light; Beyond Intellect: Opening Your Higher Mind; and Journey to the Temple of the Masters to Reprogram at Cellular. 8 processes, 4 two-sided tapes in album. All contain inaudible sound frequencies and music by Michael Hammer. *(SG200) $49.95*

Creating Money. These audio cassette prosperity tapes by Orin are for creating an abundant reality. Processes include: **Magnetizing Yourself** (SI010), **Clearing Beliefs and Old Programs** (SI071), **Releasing Doubts and Fears** (SI075), **Linking with Your Soul and the Guides** (SI076), **Aura Clearing, Energy and Lightwork** (SI073), **Awakening Your Prosperity Self** (SI074), **Success** (SI070), and **Creating Abundance** (SI072). All tapes are $9.98 each. For a set of all 8 processes (4 two-sided tapes in vinyl album), order the Creating Money Album and save. *(M100) $49.95* All contain inaudible sound frequencies and music by Michael Hammer.

LuminEssence Productions • P.O. Box 19117 • Oakland, CA 94619

Order Form

Order by Phone with Visa/Mastercard: (415) 482-4560

BUY ANY THREE TAPES FOR $9.98
GET A FOURTH $9.98 TAPE FREE!!
(Free tape offer does not apply to tape albums.)

Your Name _____

Address _____

City _____ State _____ Zip _____

Telephone: Home (_____)_____ Work (_____) _____
(In case we have any questions about your order.)

QTY	ITEM	DESCRIPTION	PRICE

POSTAGE RATES:

	First Class Mail*	U.P.S.
Up to $12 ...	$1.45	$2.50
$13 to $25 ...	$2.50	$3.00
$26 to $45 ...	$4.25	$3.50
$46 to $65 ...	$5.75	$4.00
$66 to $85 ...	$7.25	$4.50
$86 to $100 ...	$8.00	$5.75
Over $100 ...	$10.00	$7.00

*For First Class shipping of books add .50 for each book ordered.

Subtotal	
Sales tax*	
Postage	
Priority handling ($3.00)	
TOTAL	

*CA residents add appropriate sales tax.

☐ Check here if you prefer your order shipped UPS.
(UPS cannot deliver to PO Box addresses.)

Thank You for Your Order!

Payment enclosed: ☐ Check   ☐ Money Order

Please charge my: ☐ VISA   ☐ MasterCard

Credit Card No. _____ Exp. Date _____

Signature as on card _____

Please make check payable to **LuminEssence Productions**. Canadian and foreign orders payable in U.S. Funds drawn ON a U.S. Bank. Canadian and Mexican orders add $2.00 to U.S. Postage; other foreign orders add $7.50 to U.S. Postage. All international orders will be shipped by air. Regular orders will be shipped within 2 weeks of receipt; priority-handling orders will be shipped within 72 hours of receipt. Remember to allow time for U.S. Mail or UPS delivery after order is shipped. Incomplete orders will be returned.

COMPATIBLE BOOKS FROM

H J KRAMER INC

WAY OF THE PEACEFUL WARRIOR
by Dan Millman
*A story of mystery and adventure ideally suited to empower your
transformative process. Available in book and audio cassette format.*

TALKING WITH NATURE
by Michael J. Roads
A guidebook to align you with the energies of the plant and animal kingdoms.

AMAZING GRAINS: CREATING VEGETARIAN
MAIN DISHES WITH WHOLE GRAINS
by Joanne Saltzman
Amazing Grains *teaches the creative process
in cooking as well as offering delicious recipes.*

SEVENFOLD PEACE
by Gabriel Cousens, M.D.
*Based on the ancient wisdom of the Essenes,
Dr. Cousens offers a holistic approach to peace.*

JOY IN A WOOLLY COAT
by Julie Adams Church
A simple and inspiring book that provides grief support for pet loss.

JOURNEY INTO NATURE
by Michael J. Roads
*A spiritual journey in which you
will experience humanity through the eyes of nature.*

MESSENGERS OF LIGHT:
THE ANGELS' GUIDE TO SPIRITUAL GROWTH
by Terry Lynn Taylor
*A lighthearted look at the angelic kingdom
designed to help you create heaven in your life.*

YOU THE HEALER
by José Silva and Robert B. Stone
*The world-famous Silva Method will teach you to attune to
lower-frequency brain waves for use in healing.*

PURE LOVE: AFFIRMATIONS JUST FOR THIS MOMENT
by Carole A. Daxter
Pure Love *affirms your connection to a safe and friendly universe.*